More Praise for *Practicing the Preaching Life*

"I can think of no one better to lead us toward centered humility, compassionate empathy, participatory wisdom, and courageous justice than my friend and teacher, Dave Ward. His life and preaching exude these virtues. *Practicing the Preaching Life* is an invaluable resource to preachers who are interested in not just preaching well, but living well. (Re)connecting preaching with both worship and discipleship, Dave Ward reminds us that 'good preachers' are not necessarily those with the most polished skills, but rather, those men and women whose lives are marked by a handful of key virtues."
—**Steve Murrell**, founding pastor of Victory Manila in the Philippines; cofounder and president of Every Nation Churches & Ministries, based in Brentwood, TN

"David Ward has done us a great favor with this book, calling attention to the most neglected element of preaching in the modern period: the formation of the preacher's faith and life to be a faithful witness to the word of God. This holistic approach to preaching is a healthy corrective to our excessively self-interested ways. Perhaps a new generation will be guided towards recovering the joy of preaching!"
—**Michael Pasquarello III**, Methodist Chair of Divinity and director, Robert Smith Jr. Preaching Institute, Beeson Divinity School, Samford University, Birmingham, AL

"With reference both to historical and contemporary preachers and theologians, Ward charts the preacher's cultivation of the deep virtues of centered humility, compassionate empathy, participatory wisdom, and courageous justice—and shows how these deep, daily virtues bear fruit in our sermons. *Practicing the Preaching Life* provides seasoned and newbie preachers alike with spiritual refreshment and specific insights that will improve their next sermon."
—**Alyce M. McKenzie**, Le Van Professor of Preaching and Worship; Altshuler Distinguished Teaching Professor; director, The Perkins Center for Preaching Excellence, Perkins School of Theology, Southern Methodist University, Dallas, TX

"David Ward has given to us a much needed book on the preaching life and the manner in which it is related to the sermon. He has rightly adduced that good sermons give voice to good forms of life, and effective preaching is indeed more about life than it is about the perfection of a skill set. This book not only enriches the practice of preaching but it enriches the formative life of the preacher."
—**Cleophus J. LaRue Jr.**, Francis Landey Patton Professor of Homiletics, Princeton Theological Seminary, Princeton, NJ

"David Ward wisely reminds us that preaching is more than a sermon or the sum of its associated technical skills. It is a life....Preachers, if you want to live fully and joyously, read this refreshing book. Every page will urge you toward knowing that a real eloquent sermon is a life lived well before a living God."
—**Luke A. Powery**, dean, Duke University Chapel; associate professor of homiletics, Duke Divinity School, Duke University, Durham, NC

"David Ward properly locates preaching in life in very practical ways every preacher would do well to follow. The 'how to' of this book is a path to a deeper life of virtue and practice. It will change the preacher so that God's grace might flow more freely in the encounter between preacher and congregation."
—**Ken Schenck**, professor of New Testament and ancient languages; dean, School of Theology and Ministry, Indiana Wesleyan University, Marion, IN

"David Ward has written a beautiful, informed, and timely guidebook on authenticity in preaching. He is rightly concerned not with the perceived character of the preacher—Aristotle's ethos—but with actual character."
—**Paul Scott Wilson**, professor of homiletics, Emmanuel College, University of Toronto, Toronto, Ontario, Canada

DAVID B. WARD

PRACTICING THE PREACHING LIFE

Abingdon Press™

Nashville

PRACTICING THE PREACHING LIFE
Copyright © 2019 by Abingdon Press

This book is printed on acid-free paper.

Library of Congress Cataloging-in-Publication Data has been requested.

ISBN 978-1-5018-5494-1

19 20 21 22 23 24 25 26 27 28—10 9 8 7 6 5 4 3 2 1
MANUFACTURED IN THE UNITED STATES OF AMERICA

For Holly,
Ella, Zoe, and Dawson—
my skylights and refrains

Contents

Contents

Chapter 8

Chapter 9

ACKNOWLEDGMENTS

The kindnesses we receive along a journey multiply over time. There are some whose memory endures, whose influence strengthens, and whose meaning deepens. These are the kind one wants to signal to the world, to acknowledge as an encouragement to us all to be like them. Of course, dearest Holly, your sacrifices to help me get away and your cheerful editing pale in comparison only to how easy you make it to come home. Keith Drury, you have been a life guide, a friend, a colleague, and a winsome preaching voice in my ears for twenty years. I think you know who you are to me. Paul Hontz, your preaching disciplines are a part of me, as are you. Cleo LaRue, Jim Kay, Mike Pasquarello, Michael Brothers, Sally Brown, Gordon Mikoski, and Luke Powery, you each led me to intellectual caves full of many treasures.

To Connie Stella, my editor with Abingdon Press, your belief in this project is a gift to me and to the devoted pastors it will serve for years to come. Thank you also to Laurie Vaughen and Suzanne Austin who caught not only paragraphs and main ideas but also left no footnote unturned. Whatever mistakes remain are due only to my prolific capacity to multiply them while attempting to fix them.

My writing companions, John Drury and Ken Schenck, did more than make somewhere else feel like home. You made writing feel like Christmas. I owe Ken, as my dean, and the School of Theology and Ministry a debt of gratitude for the sabbatical that helped this book cross the finish line. Patrick Johnson, you were the one who told me this was the horse to ride. I am still listening.

Acknowledgments

To the pastors who have trusted me with their time, their ministry, and their longing to strengthen their preaching I am indebted. Your questions have taught me, your ideas helped others, and this book really is for you. David Vardaman, thirty years of pastoring made your advice and encouragement invaluable to me. Pastor Denor, Pastor Doucet, and the rest of the Haitian preachers who came to La Gonave, you showed me so clearly how time was the beginning of all preaching challenges. To Deech and the Center for Youth Ministry training, your comments helped me realize how much pastors of all kinds need new sermon forms for new preaching wine. Pastors Nixon, Manny, and Steve, I could thank you for uplifted faith, increased joy in the gospel, or for introducing me to such an empowering model of preaching. Instead, as with all the above, I thank you most for your friendship.

Let's keep preaching together, never alone.

INTRODUCTION
Preaching for Life, Life for Preaching

It was two in the morning and my phone's ring was tolling. I knew who would be on the other end of the line. "Hello, Delores. I am so glad you called." I drove the twenty-five-minute route to her home I had traveled so often those last two months. I led the family in singing "Amazing Grace" into the dark, holding hands around the bed of Delores's husband as he passed from this life into the arms of God. I stayed a little longer to hear a few stories. Each ended with tears, laughter, or both. Ed was lifeless a few feet away. We held his hand and kissed him goodbye. I had fished with him two weeks before. That Sunday, I preached.

A few months later I visited the hospital in the middle of the day as Tom and Wendy had welcomed their new hopes and fears into the world, wrapping her in a striped hospital blanket. Another sermon found voice that Sunday.

My earliest preaching memories were surrounded by life's joys and tragedies, meaningfully shared with others. Looking backward, there was nothing intentional about this. Unwittingly, this early season of ministry was teaching me to love the pastoring and preaching life as a mutually enriching unity.

Years later, a seminary student asked to meet with me after class. "Preparing to preach demoralizes me," he said. I did not understand until he showed me his preaching preparation process and the book that taught it to him. It was a process separated from life in ways I had never known.

It was birthed in books, was dressed on paper, and never found breath until the Sunday morning hour. No wonder it demoralized.

In another setting, I was the listener and a well-known preacher was preaching to pastors. In a room full of hopeful and eager preachers, his stories and quips and jokes were met with audible and visible acceptance. When he reached the climactic delivery of his core message he told us with conviction, "Never say good enough . . . never ever say good enough." His moralizing and high standard pressed a burdensome "must" upon many shoulders. His listeners left with the sense that being faithful was equated with achieving perfection. Preachers were called not to practice but to perfect. The drive to perfect necessarily requires preachers to retreat from life and ministry and block out inordinate amounts of time for preparation. Yet again preaching was disconnected from life.

Good preaching breathes the air of life. We cannot separate the speaking of sermons from the living of days. If all is going well, sermons are born from life and give birth to new life. For this reason, we do not live to hear the casual words, "Good sermon, pastor." Those words are often accompanied by limp handshakes and thin smiles anyway. The aim of preaching is not a good sermon, and certainly not a perfect one. A good sermon is not a bad thing. Preaching simply holds a longer view and a higher trajectory than a sermon. The aim of preaching is living well as a worshipping community for the sake of the world. For anyone studying preaching then, the conclusion is clear. Preaching's first question is not "What makes a good sermon?" The first question is "What makes a good life?" In between the good life and the good sermon stands the living preacher. This book is about the preaching life and how to live it well.

Perhaps, you are already disturbed by these thoughts. Good sermons are at least helpful, are they not? Church attenders grow weary of boring, dry, strung-out, abstract, or moralistic sermons. Good sermons are important, perhaps more important than ever. Yet what makes them good? Is it a tight form or well-spun phrases? Is it imagistic words that layer paint onto the canvas of the mind? Or is it stories that evoke tears and rolling laughter? If these things form the deepest level of good we can imagine, our vision of the good is shortsighted. These skills are good, truly good, but not deeply so. Good sermons that are good way down deep give voice to good forms of life. They are more than sermon structures, images, and stories. They can even be the living word of God because God chooses to make them so. Good sermons are living, breathing, and pulsing testimonies of grace.

You may also think of broken preachers as cracked pots whose fractures seem to deliver grace all the more generously. Is living the preaching life well judged by flawless performance of moral codes? Or is it about a checklist of pietistic rituals? If sermons are to be living, breathing, and pulsing testimonies of grace, then flawless preachers do not match the medium. Grace is not needed for flawless people. Instead, it is the participation in the grace of God that makes the preacher a living Word, an embodied voice of hope. At the same time, grace abused leads to images we wrestle with such as "Father Oprah" and his fall from grace with a bikini-clad companion on the beaches of Florida some years ago.[1] Preachers do not need to be perfect exemplars of Christian practice. Instead, good preachers long to be well-practiced participants in the life of God.

One of Christianity's most striking theological claims is that preachers are living voices of the living Word. The threefold nature of the Word (Christ, Scripture, and Proclamation) indicates preaching becomes the Word of God for us because God chooses to make it so. The Word of God functions through the Spirit of God to call out a people, to redeem and restore that people, and to put a love for the world in their hearts. Our preaching, therefore, is not aimed at an end-in-itself of good preaching. The end goal of preaching is the ongoing formation of the Christian community, including the preacher, into increasing congruence with the gospel as a "being-saved community" in and for the world.[2] Congruence with the gospel is not moralistic but grace-centered and world-conscious. This places preaching in an even larger context than human life: the life of God. Our practicing of the preaching life can therefore be, if we

---

1. Father Oprah and a number of other illustrative instances from both sides of abusing grace are described poignantly in Robert Stephen Reid, ed., *Slow of Speech and Unclean Lips: Contemporary Images of Preaching Identity* (Eugene, OR: Wipf and Stock, 2010).

2. David Buttrick, *Homiletic: Moves and Structures* (Philadelphia: Fortress Press, 1988), 14–16, 246–47. Particularly attractive is Buttrick's statement that "Christians may be termed being-saved communities insofar as in the midst of human brokenness they may display signs of a new quality of life and have some awareness that they represent a different social reality in the world" (p. 254).

receive this grace, an imperfect parable of participating in the life of God. Imperfection and beauty are not separated. They go hand in hand. A preaching life, though imperfect, can be a beautiful life.

All I wish to describe in this book is how preachers can preach from and to life while living all of life within the life of God. At first glance, the topic is modest. One sentence contains it all. Yet, with any reflection, it is audacious. Preaching is more about life than it is about skills. The true preaching life is one swept up into the redeeming life of God. Sermons are always about divine participation in human life and a human participation in divine life. In order to proclaim it well, we must be swept up in it. When we are swept up into it, our best skills are virtuously used. Then preaching is truly good. Seeking to form a preaching life that is truly good is much more difficult than teaching people to write a good sermon or two, as difficult as teaching sermon crafting often seems.

Viewing preaching as embedded in life creates a spiral of formation, a chicken and an egg. Which comes first? Good preaching or good living? The moralists among us will insist it is good living. "Only preach what you practice," they may say. Yet, that reverses the time-worn saying "Practice what you preach." The last time I practiced something it was for a jazz piece I had not played in years on the piano. It was very far from perfect. I cannot play what I practice, until I have practiced what I wish to play. If preachers had to master the piece of life they were proclaiming before they could proclaim it, we would rarely hear a sermon in church.

The advocates of grace alone will say that good preaching comes first and there is no other requirement. In part, they are right. Works righteousness is just as damaging now as it has always been. Even though nothing more than grace is required, there is a difference between what is necessary and what is better. Preachers long to choose what is better. Cheap grace, to use Bonhoeffer's phrase, is no more admirable than moralizing is. When I describe the practice of preaching as a preaching life, I am suggesting that the circle of formation is not divisible. The life of the preacher and the preaching life are intertwined. We know this as true in our bones even if we defend against it to make a theological or anthropological point. Further, the preacher's life does not exist in isolation. The community of faith and the person of the preacher mutually affect each other. Deciding which comes first is a futile effort.

For this book, the preacher's formation in community is my starting point simply because this is a book about preaching for preachers. However, the formation of the preacher in community cannot be examined without paying attention to the formation of Christian community. That which forms us, we also form. This spiral between preacher and community also lives within a larger tension of church and world. Formation for the sake of an insular community is not congruent with a gospel that is for the world. The preacher is formed in Christian community; the community is formed in and for the world. The world's needs compel the preacher to speak and so to help form the community. This community is not shaped for itself, but for the sake of the world.[3] As in every ethical consideration, agent and environment, individual and society, culture and other cultures, local and global are indivisibly interwoven. We only distinguish them to understand them.

Though there have been preaching texts in the last hundred years of homiletical theory that have focused on preaching as a way of life,[4] even a communal practice, the voices of these texts have been drowned out by more numerous and more popular texts that zero in on the skills and techniques necessary to produce the weekly sermon.[5] Many of these texts could echo Craddock's statement in his textbook *Preaching*: "The structure of this book is an attempt to answer the question 'How do I

---

3. Sally A. Brown and Luke A. Powery, *Ways of the Word: Learning to Preach for Your Time and Place* (Minneapolis: Fortress Press, 2016). Brown and Powery consistently call for a world-focused gospel in preaching. Preaching all too often becomes in-turned and sectarian in both diction and direction.

4. Some examples might include Michael Pasquarello III, *Sacred Rhetoric: Preaching as a Theological and Pastoral Practice of the Church* (Grand Rapids, MI: William B. Eerdmans, 2002) and John S. McClure, *Other-wise Preaching: A Postmodern Ethic for Homiletics* (St. Louis: Chalice Press, 2001). McClure states that when we live what he is suggesting as other-wise preaching it is "a saintly nonviolent act with, for, and on behalf of others. Perhaps this is to reassert the profound connection between preaching and a way of life" (p. 150). A more recent virtue-focused work is Lucy Lind Hogan's *Graceful Speech: An Invitation to Preaching* (Louisville, KY: Westminster John Knox Press, 2006).

5. See Eugene Lowry, *The Homiletical Plot: The Sermon as Narrative Art Form*, rev. ed. (Louisville, KY: Westminster John Knox Press, 2001); Fred Craddock, *Preaching* (Nashville: Abingdon Press, 1985); and Thomas G. Long, *The Witness of Preaching* (Louisville, KY: Westminster John Knox Press, 2005). These are three of the most often quoted or used. Many of the rest will appear in coming pages.

prepare and deliver a sermon?'"[6] Craddock's book is representative not only of this emphasis on a single sermon but also of the resulting superior position given to skills and techniques in reflections on preaching. Skills and techniques are not the enemy of preaching. Placing them in a position of first priority is.

There are a few poetic voices on the margin. Brief though beautiful essays such as Marva Dawn's "Not *What* but *Who* Is the Matter with Preaching?" stand on the periphery of skill-centered preaching books and deliver a prophetic word.[7] We need to heed that word and find a new way home for our preaching. Whatever way we find will be worthy of our efforts insofar as it is shaped by good news, new opportunities, wide horizons, and ever-increasing capacity to enjoy loving God and neighbor. This book provides at least one other way: practicing the preaching life.

Preaching is a formative Christian practice. As one of many Christian practices it cycles between the life of faith and the proclamation of faithful life in ways that form both preacher and community. This cycle of doing and saying both strengthens and requires certain virtues for preaching that preachers instinctively desire. Preachers preach from life to life, cycling between skill and virtue formation in organic unity as well as between the practice of preaching and the other practices of the faith.[8] Every preacher I know longs for preaching to be life giving for them and the worshipping community. Unfortunately, many preachers experience it as anxious, burdensome, and emptying. There is another way. It is a way in which preaching is embedded in a life shaped by Christian practices. Preaching then emerges as one practice supported by many. The preaching life is woven together with the life of faith in mutually energizing ways.

Practicing the preaching life well makes sermon creation emerge naturally from the person of the preacher and the life of the community of

---

6. Craddock, *Preaching*, 15. Craddock discusses "the life of study" in 6 of the 224 pages (pp. 69–75). This section is dwarfed in comparison to the sections on the sermon in context, the selection of the text, shaping the message into a sermon, the formation of a sermon, and delivering the sermon (notice the recurrence of singular articles).

7. Mark Graves, ed., *What's the Matter with Preaching Today?* (Louisville, KY: Westminster John Knox Press, 2004), 75–91.

8. Chapter 2, "What Preaching Does Best," addresses the unity of skill and virtue in some detail. Chapter 5, "Practicing a Christian Life," focuses on this interconnected web of Christian practices.

faith. This book will not begin with the skills and steps necessary for moving from text to sermon. Instead, it will help the preacher discover the kind of person and form of life that help a minister develop and preach sermons organically, joyfully, and graciously. This book will help guide your longing, shape your being, and direct your doing as a preacher in congruence with the gospel. Then the skills of preaching will find their natural home.

During Advent a member of our church organized a singing of carols at a local Christian assisted-living center. The climactic moment was the gathering in the cafeteria. As we were singing "Silent Night" one old soul's wild eyes seemed to try to catch mine. I made eye contact and smiled. She shouted, "Stop it! Stop it!" The leader of our little merry band walked over while still singing to try and calm the dissenter. All the louder she cried, "Why don't you listen to the words you're singing!" A care worker emerged and came to pacify, but the lady continued, "How can you sing of peace on earth when..." and I lost the words in the sound of the song around me.

All Advent and into Christmastide those eyes and words remained with me. Naturally, I listened more to the lyrics we sang. Bombs were dropping in Syria. Explosions were ripping Baghdad. Untried Arab civilians remained in US custody. Civil war raged on in Africa. An Iranian American pastor faced hanging. All during that season we sang phrases such as "Silent Night" and "Peace on Earth." The preaching texts were already chosen. Yet now, with her eyes in mind, the step toward my upcoming sermon introduction seemed obvious, even alive. "How is it that we can sing of peace on earth," I would ask, "when bombs are dropping in Syria, explosions are puncturing Baghdad...?" The sermon process was now intimately connected to life and death. Suddenly the preaching of this text became more than a need to produce a sermon. It became an expression of life speaking to life—in the face of death. It was accomplished through fragmented attempts toward humility, empathy, and wisdom ruptured by a yearning desire for justice.

The above practice of visiting the sick and infirm is not separate from preaching. Other examples from the experience of the life of faith in community could be used ad infinitum. Hopefully this one vignette will serve to gesture toward the direction of this book. The practice of the Christian life and the preparation of a Christian sermon is organically intertwined. Paul's loving words to his former church resonate with all the pastors I know: "We were glad to share not only God's good news with you but also our very lives because we cared for you so much" (1 Thess 2:18). We preach from life to life, and we therefore necessarily include our lives as well and seek to make our lives well in the process. Imagine how good it would be if the preaching life to which you are called also was a good life, a beautiful life, and a life that helped to make and keep you well. That kind of preaching life would be worth practicing for its own sake.

CHAPTER 1
What Makes a Practice Good?

My children get the opportunity to live in a neighborhood with people of various racial and ethnic descents: African American, Haitian, Philippine, Caucasian, Puerto Rican, Russian, Indian, and others. What a joy that is. All of this is on one street in one neighborhood, in a relatively rural town. If the preaching of the church they go to is to reach even their single street, it will need to find ways to address a diverse context in a singular place. Certainly, a beautiful opportunity for the preaching life today is the intermingling of cultures all over the world. This opportunity also presents a question for how to preach well and how to know when we have preached well. Where do we find the standards for preaching to such diverse contexts when standards differ from place to place, community to community, and culture to culture? How do we guide preachers who will not only preach to contexts that are diverse but also need to preach in a diversity of contexts over their preaching ministry? In short, we have some difficult questions to ask of preaching, or any practice, in this season of human history.

Who gets to decide what makes preaching better? And who is it better for once the definition of "better" is decided? If you are reading a preaching book you most likely want to be a good preacher, not just craft one good sermon. That requires a practice of preaching that meets diverse contexts with consistent goodness. *What makes the practice of preaching truly good across cultures and contexts?* Answering the question well requires more than learning seventeen culturally specific ways to preach. Learning to preach to different but discrete cultures is important. Yet, all seventeen of those cultures may be present in the same service.

For the sake of an analogy, imagine that you want to build a neighborhood. What goes into building a good house? There are some components that will be true of any structure we deem a house. The stability, security, shelter, and unity of the dwelling will likely all come into view. However, for a good house to be a truly good house it has to be good for those who dwell in it. A portion of that will be highly culturally determined.

Preaching is a practice, but it is also like a home, a place we have to live. A clear picture of the working parts any practice has will help us make sure the most important components are all in working order. To that end this chapter outlines the most important characteristics of practices that persist in any context: aim, functions, external versus internal goods, and virtues. Think of these as building codes for constructing your preaching house. Like building codes, this chapter may be more difficult to understand than the actual building of the thing itself (such as using a sermon form in chapter 9). Yet these codes can prevent the house from being unethically constructed, unsafe, or inhospitable in coming years. The next two chapters will gather the wisdom of the ages of homiletics to describe what it looks like when these working parts are in good order for the practice of preaching. (See appendix C for an illustration of all components working together.) For now, we need to know what a practice is and how practices are culturally modified: how does a homiletics house becomes a suitable preaching home?

Practices Defined

A violinist, a tennis player, and a chess player practice their performance. Though preachers do need to practice their skill sets in this way at times, it is not the sense of the term "practice" theologians typically intend. We are pointing toward a more holistic use of the term when we talk of *practicing* the preaching life. The sociological and philosophical exploration of practices and the technical meaning of the word *practice* was initiated primarily by two very different thinkers: Pierre Bourdieu and Alasdair MacIntyre.[1] Both MacIntyre's *After Virtue*[2] and Bourdieu's *Outline of a Theory of Practice*[3] offer influential views of formation through habitual practices. Each of them offers something unique to how we understand preaching as a practice that shapes our lives.

MacIntyre helps define the aspects of practice this book prescribes for preachers: what preaching does best, how it does it well, and what kind of person is required to enjoy the preaching life. Bourdieu describes the aspects of practice against which this book warns: insensitive standards based on ignorance of class and cultural differences. Both of these poles are needed for a whole and healthy picture of the practice of preaching to emerge.

First, MacIntyre's definitions and categories help us define the important components of a well-ordered practice of preaching. MacIntyre defines a practice as a "meaningful, coherent, and complex set of actions pursued communally over time for goods internal to the practice."[4] We pursue preaching and other practices first and foremost for the sake of the good that is possible through those practices. Though preaching can be seen in all of its complexity (performative, rhetorical, theological, exegetical, and liturgical), it is one practice pursued across the ages for the sake of the common good. The complex practice of preaching has survived for millennia because it persistently accomplishes good when we practice preaching well. Further, as we will explore below, preaching accomplishes good for preacher and listener, individual and community, through the good things that naturally emerge within and around preaching. Those

---

1. Ludwig Wittgenstein's view of practices is also very influential. However, Wittgenstein is concerned with the use and meaning of words. Bourdieu and MacIntyre focus more on the meaning and use of practices than words (though they are inseparable). See Wittgenstein, *Philosophical Investigations*, 3rd ed., trans. Gertrude Elisabeth Margaret Anscombe (New York: McMillan, 1971).

2. Alasdair MacIntyre, *After Virtue: A Study in Moral Theory*, 2nd ed. (Notre Dame, IN: University of Notre Dame Press, 1984). The categories MacIntyre offers are helpful; his narrative of decline is not necessarily as helpful. It is perhaps a narrative of cultural resentment and longing for a previous, less diverse time.

3. Pierre Bourdieu, *Outline of a Theory of Practice*, trans. R. Nice (Cambridge: Cambridge University Press, 1977), 72. Originally published as Pierre Bourdieu, *Esquisse d'une théorie de la pratique, précédé de Trois édtudes d'ethnologie kabyle* (Geneve: Droz, 1972).

4. MacIntyre, *After Virtue*, 187.

good things preaching accomplishes can be divided between either internal or external goods.

Internal goods are those goods that reside within the practice itself. These goods are accomplished by pursuing the practice over time according to its appropriate standards. When we practice well, good things happen naturally and intrinsically. Part of what distinguishes practices from other activities is the shared nature of their internal goods. As MacIntyre puts it, "It is characteristic of [practices] that their achievement is a good for the whole community who participate in the practice."[5] Inspiration toward love and good deeds through a preaching life is a communally shared good; the pastor's expense fund or paycheck is not. The opportunity to give witness to the goodness of God is an internal good; the preacher's national reputation is not. The enjoyment of God through the worshipful description of God's character is an internal good; the building of a larger church is not. The internal goods are good in an intrinsic way. There is good in receiving a paycheck, a good reputation, and a growing church if all things are in balance. These are simply a different kind of good: external.

External goods are those goods that are attached to practices from the outside by social convention or social accident. Salaries, positions, bonuses, products held in hand, winning or losing, status, prestige, or power are all external goods. External goods can degrade a practice when the practice is pursued primarily for their sake. External goods are goods only inasmuch as they are seen as peripheral, and secondary to the internal goods of the practice. At the same time, a sensible balance between external and internal goods is required for practices to endure.[6]

When things get out of balance it affects our sense of the goodness of the practice, can diminish the community's enjoyment of the goods attached to the practice, and often calls the practice into question as a

---

5. Ibid., 190–91.

6. Paul Hager, "Refurbishing MacIntyre's Account of Practice," *Journal of Philosophy of Education* 45, no. 3 (August 2011): 545–61. I agree with Hager's critique of MacIntyre's tendency to denigrate external goods. MacIntyre helpfully highlights the damaging results of focusing on external goods as primary pursuits. Hager modifies MacIntyre's tendency toward cynical idealism by calling attention to MacIntyre's more lucid moments when he recognizes the necessity of external goods (money, position, and so forth) for institutional maintenance of practices.

whole. If the external goods are ignored, the core practitioners (preachers in this case) can feel used and even abused. If the external goods become central, the community can feel used and even abused.

For example, preaching's goodness is not primarily bound up in pay, reputation, or even influence. Still, preaching must give attention to these things with a degree of wisdom and communal concern. These things are not evil, but necessary and good when in right perspective. Preachers do well to always remember that a salary is an external good (therefore not the focus) but still good (therefore not to be demeaned, dismissed, or denied). A worker is worth his wages (1 Tim 5:18). Bi-vocational ministry is to be affirmed but not required or idealized. It is good for a preacher to decide to preach for free on occasion or for good reason; it is not good for a community with resources to ask him to do so. In short, it is best when external goods serve internal goods but do not become the primary motive.

Particularly in Protestant preaching traditions, preaching has been recognized to have a particular kind of good nature given to it by God. It is not merely a practice with internal goods we enjoy and external goods that sustain it. All practices can be described this way. Preaching is also sacramental insofar as God has ordained it, graced it, and brings grace through it. The practice of preaching is good not just because it makes sense. Paul names preaching foolishness, after all. The practice of preaching is good because God in God's sovereign grace makes it so.

As a result, prayer is not a footnote for preaching. Prayerful engagement with the sacramental nature of preaching is the only authentic way for preaching to be practiced. *Preaching is one way of practicing prayer, and prayer is life-giving to all stages of preaching.* Even poor preaching can accomplish good when God wills it. Truth be told, prayer-less preaching can accomplish good as well. It simply is not as good for the preacher.

Praying for preaching need not be anxious or fearful. God is merciful and will bring a living word. The communal experience of this answer to prayer is an internal good. A congregation's affirmation of the preacher because of God's faithfulness through preaching is an external good. Distinguishing between internal and external goods helps us avoid self-inflicted martyrdom on the one hand and self-serving vices on the other.

How we relate to preaching's external goods, internal goods, and other preachers can be habitually praiseworthy or habitually lamentable as well. Certain habitual ways of being, most often called virtues, are both required for and formed by the healthy enjoyment of internal goods of a practice. MacIntyre's explicit definition of *virtue* reads this way: "A virtue is an acquired human quality the possession and the exercise of which tends to enable us to achieve those goods which are internal to practices and the lack of which effectively prevents us from achieving any such goods."[7]

A practice is not an ultimate cause of attitudes and virtues. It is possible to engage in a practice in such a way that the practitioner is not more virtuous but more vicious.[8] Consider the prejudiced preacher proclaiming hatred or the nationalistic preacher prioritizing a nation's prosperity over justice for the poor. However, pursuing a practice in the right way turns attitudes into actions, actions into habits, and habitual attitudes and habitual actions into what many call virtues.

If we named the internal goods, external goods, and virtues of the preaching life we would miss something very crucial. What is the aim or purpose of it all? Does preaching exist simply to help worshipping communities enjoy being good and the good things that come from being good? This is a rather small and self-obsessed view for preaching to hold. All of the above elements are necessary to carry the practitioner along in the quest for the ultimate *aim* of the practice that points to something outside of preaching itself.[9] In a central statement for his work MacIntyre claims these virtues enable the practice and the lifelong pursuit of the greater good through the practices:

---

7. MacIntyre, *After Virtue*, 188.

8. See Elizabeth Frazer and Nicola Lacey's essay "MacIntyre, Feminism and the Concept of Practice," in *After MacIntyre: Critical Perspectives on the Work of Alasdair MacIntyre*, ed. John Horton and Susan Mendus (Notre Dame, IN: University of Notre Dame Press, 1994), 265–80. Frazer and Lacey raise the specter of "evil practices" (p. 267) such as rape, battery, and the unequal distribution of food and work. MacIntyre responds that when these things occur they are not evil practices per se but activities pursued out of vice, even practices pursued viciously (p. 290). Whether or not his response is correct, the warning is needed: *practices are not guarantees of good.*

9. MacIntyre, *After Virtue*, 218–19. *Telos* is the word used by MacIntyre.

> The virtues therefore are to be understood as those dispositions which will not only sustain practices and enable us to achieve the goods internal to practice, but which will also sustain us in the relevant kind of quest for the good, by enabling us to overcome the harms, dangers, temptations and distractions which we encounter and which will furnish us with increasing self-knowledge and increasing knowledge of the good.[10]

Reading the person of the preacher from the perspective of practices and virtues, the preacher will find herself as one of the "bearers of a tradition" that has its own history in the form of a quest for the good.[11] This aim, purpose, or ultimate good takes preaching beyond itself and sends worshipping communities beyond themselves toward something greater that benefits all of humanity, not only those who enjoy the practice of preaching.

Understanding preaching as a Christian practice can help preachers realize that preaching is a virtue-sustained and virtue-sustaining practice that serves an ultimate end beyond itself. In this way, preaching's goods are not strictly internal to the practice itself. Neither are preacher's goods purely external in a material way. *The ultimate aim of preaching must be something that benefits the world, not only the church.*

The concepts of aim, internal goods, external goods, and virtues give us a strong framework to understand preaching as a practice. Still, something crucial is missing from the picture of practices if we are to understand them clearly. The missing component is the *functions* of the practice.[12] Preaching is not a "product." A "sermon" is not the primary focus of preaching. Certainly, the text of a sermon is hardly worth calling a sermon since a sermon is a live event. Even a video of a sermon without a listener is at best a stored sermon waiting to be reopened by a listener and enlivened by God. Preaching is a practice that exists among God, the preacher, and the listening community. Yet even if we described

---

10. Ibid., 219. This section qualifies his earlier definition of virtues to include gleanings from the medieval concept of quest.

11. Ibid., 220.

12. The functions of the practice of preaching are related to but different from the function of a particular sermon. Thomas Long's outstanding introduction to preaching, *The Witness of Preaching*, suggests preachers craft a function statement answering the question, What does the sermon seek to do to the listener? (Louisville, KY: Westminster John Knox Press, 2005), 108–10.

the aim, virtues, and goods of preaching we would be left with a very important question for any preacher: "What exactly does the practice of preaching do?"

We know that preaching does something. It is hard to define and nail down, and yet most believe they know it when they have experienced it. "Now that was good preaching," we say. Or in some traditions, "Now that was church." The aim of preaching does not define what preaching does in the moment. It defines what preaching accomplishes over time. Good preaching does something. It functions in particular ways in Christian community, and the hallmarks of those functions can be defined. *A function is an activity for which a thing is specially fitted.* If we only discern a practice's aim (purpose or telos), and then look for its goods and virtues, there is a large gap between. This is important for discussions of preaching since disagreements on the purpose of preaching or its aim are contentious and seem to have no resolution.[13] Part of the reason for this disagreement is the lack of distinction between the categories of aim and function. If the aim of preaching (its vision of ultimate good) and the functions of preaching (those tasks preaching is well fitted to accomplish) are distinguished from each other, then it is easier to have clear discussion regarding the aim of preaching. All practices are better understood when aims, virtues, goods, and functions are clearly in view. This holistic view defines the building codes of practices. It does not yet define the particular kind of house of homiletics. Nor does it make clear what kind of homiletics house a particular culture or context may prefer.

So far, this chapter provides a lens for understanding preaching as a Christian practice. Preachers will do well to learn the aim, functions, internal goods, external goods, and virtues of preaching. These will guide the preacher in forming a good life, not merely producing a good sermon. In other words, these are the building codes gathered by homiletics over time that we follow for our own good. It is the preaching life, the life of the congregation, and the life of the world that is always in view for good

---

13. For an amiable example of this disagreement, see the collection of essays on the purpose of preaching edited by Jana Childers, *Purposes of Preaching* (St. Louis: Chalice Press, 2004). The conflicting accounts of the purpose of preaching are easily seen by comparing two essays such as John S. McClure's "Preaching and the Redemption of Language" and Paul Scott Wilson's "Preaching as a Theological Venture." Chapter 2 distinguishes preaching's aims from its functions.

preaching, not merely the production of a single sermon. The question of diversity, contexts, cultures, and the difficulty of who decides what makes things good, better, and best remains. How can a preacher best preach to the diverse inhabitants of my street? For that, we need a new conversation partner.

Culture and the Preaching Life

There is a blindness that afflicts preachers. After years of seeing the congregation week after week, it is easy to miss the differences among the seats or even the diverse congregation that is not yet there.[14] Preaching best reaches those whom the preacher sees and understands. As a result, it is a grave danger to preaching when a preacher is blind to others or calloused to another's world. In contrast to MacIntyre's emphasis on context-transcending descriptions of practices, Bourdieu focuses on the context-dependent nature of class, gender, ethnicity, and other contextual components of practices. Instead of discussing virtues Bourdieu discusses *habitus* or "systems of durable, transposable *dispositions*."[15]

Disposition is a word often used interchangeably with *virtue*, which means that Bourdieu sees the *habitus* as a nebula of ways of being, a web of "virtues" that makes a community's way of life discernible and distinct. This *habitus* is a present past. In other words, the past experiences of the community live on as they form and structure the present. Individual actors are neither free from the class *habitus* nor robots controlled by it. We are neither completely free nor completely bound by the way our communities have shaped us. Preachers are formed by their memories of experiences within and outside of their own social location. As preachers step into the pulpit, they are surrounded by a great cloud of witnesses whose internalized voices and present faces guide them in how to go about preaching. In at least this way, we never preach alone.

---

14. The increasing prevalence of multisite churches, campus churches, and the use of technology in these campuses has the potential to make this blindness all the more common.

15. Bourdieu, *Outline of a Theory of Practice*, 72. Language of dispositions is not alien to McIntyre either but is not the primary nomenclature of the work.

Bourdieu's *habitus* is culturally formed, contextually rooted, and class oriented in its nature. While individuals are able to improvise within the practice, the *habitus* or communally shaped way of being is the "generating principle" that gives sense to the actions of the practitioner. This comes with a sort of automatic recognition to others of the same class or group.[16] Those of the same context-specific subgroup would recognize the signals of *habitus*-driven behavior and automatically find them sensible and good. The preacher who preaches extemporaneously at home and receives enthusiastic reception is surprised by the cool response elsewhere where manuscripts are the norm. Simple catch phrases bring positive responses in one culture and rejection in another. Consider these phrases as you think of diverse contexts: "Can I get an *Amen*?" "God is in control." "Turn to your neighbor and repeat after me...." "When we are at table...." "The altar is open." If you have experienced preaching in diverse contexts enough you can think of fitting and jarring contexts for each phrase. If you cannot think of a fitting or a jarring context for each phrase then perhaps your preaching experience has been more narrow than you know.

This definition of *habitus* and the attendant dispositions to the *habitus* help make sense of the great diversity of standards for "good" preaching across socioeconomic and cultural lines. It also allows room for complicating the inherited *habitus* as a potentially oppressive way of being.[17] Sometimes emerging and experienced preachers need to be helped to transcend the way of being they have been given. *Simply because something is natural to a preacher does not mean it is good.* Just because it is common "in my context" does not mean it is liberating, helpful, or life giving to the preacher or listener. There are, after all, cultural contexts in which religious shaming is common. There are also cultural contexts in which sermons regularly avoid saying anything to unsettle the society. Neither

---

16. Ibid., 72–74. This generating principle is a "strategy-generating principle" by which Bourdieu means that the socialized agent's strategies only appear to be determined by the future as they are greatly conditioned by the socialized past. This does not for Bourdieu rule out agency or it might be labeled a restrictive principle rather than generative. This generative principle gives a social player a "feel for the game," allowing for endless improvisations for even unconscious ends.

17. Ibid., 188–93.

of these is good, no matter how natural they seem to the members of the community.

However, knowing which parts of a communal way of being (*habitus*) to change for a minister's preaching is not as easy as it may seem. This is like telling someone with different tastes how to turn her house into a home: prescribing color schemes, decor, even placement of the furniture. Theological critique of cultural norms is crucial not just for preaching but for practical theology in general. At one and the same time the practical theologian must recognize the contextual nature of "good practice" and give space for evaluation of practices in diverse contexts. Preachers must respond to culture and work across cultures, attend to and transcend context, and recognize and validate social classes. This is a more textured way of saying we "become all things to all people" without losing our own culture, context, or social location.[18] Ministers do not need to be pleasers who lose their sense of self in order to be good preachers. This is perhaps the most difficult part of good preaching: testifying well to people who feel like "home," while resonating deeply with those who shake the preacher's view of the world, or pronounce life differently.

Though we can speak of a broad tradition of Christian preaching in the singular, we must realize that Christian tradition is itself made up of traditions of preaching in the plural. Each of these traditions is made of complex webs of diversity: geographical, chronological, sociocultural, socioeconomical, racial, theological, gender, and so forth. Preachers will be best served when they become aware enough and adaptable enough for their preaching ministry to cross over class, culture, ethnicity, theological traditions, and other divides. Preachers do not need to add contextual callousness to the stumbling stone of the gospel. It is difficult enough to believe.

It is also difficult to admit how much our close relationships subconsciously shape our view of each character trait we prize.[19] A preacher does

---

18. Extended guidance on preaching to particular diverse contexts requires more than one book. Two good books to begin are James R. Nieman and Thomas G. Rogers, *Preaching to Every Pew: Cross-Cultural Strategies* (Minneapolis: Fortress Press, 2002) and Matthew D. Kim, *Communicating with Cultural Intelligence: Understanding the People Who Hear Our Sermons* (Grand Rapids, MI.: Baker Academic, 2018).

19. Dialect is the most obvious form of this phenomenon, then dress. Sermon lengths, sermon forms, and movement of the preacher can all fall into this category as well. There are deeper perceived "wrongs"

not act on her or his own as an individual but is unconsciously guided by a way of being (*habitus*) inherited from her or his past. The level of improvisation available to a practitioner as a socialized preacher, his or her strategic individual action, exists within the boundaries of the larger communal *habitus*. The preacher can press the boundaries of what she has become accustomed to, but to go outside the bounds completely would be too frightful of a thing and can be experienced as "wrong."[20] That feeling of wrong is often what we call a *vice* and the feeling of right is often what we call *virtue*. The preservation of these ways of being (*habitus*) as the guide for behavior signals to the "home" community that the preacher is still trustworthy, still "one of us," and has not "forgotten where she came from."

It is an aggressive thing to grind out the culturally appropriate ways of being a preacher has inherited. It may even be an act of "symbolic violence."[21] Professors, preaching coaches, and mentors often subconsciously conceal the power dynamics involved in a rejection of that way of being. It is helpful and appropriate for teachers of preaching and lead pastors to raise this *habitus* to the level of conscious awareness so that preachers may critique their own way of being with their own familiarity of the contextual way of being they inherited.

Many white preachers, for example, are simply not aware that speaking more quietly and slowly while making significant points is a particularly white thing to do. In contrast, minority students attending white-dominated seminaries often face cultural blindness and ignorant critique in the preaching classroom particularly when they behave in the opposite way. The good and necessary actions for preaching in home communities are critiqued and marked down in theological education. If

---

that are socially formed than these. For more on the emotional and social controlling power of these dynamics see Jonathan Haidt, *The Righteous Mind: Why Good People Are Divided by Politics and Religion* (New York: Vintage Books, 2013).

20. For a work that helps us press into more cross-cultural improvisation than comes easily, see Jared Alcántara, *Crossover Preaching: Intercultural-Improvisational Homiletics in Conversation with Gardner C. Taylor* (Downers Grove, IL: Intervarsity Press, 2015).

21. Pierre Bourdieu and Jean Claude Passeron, *Reproduction in Education, Society, and Culture*. 2nd edition, trans. Richard Nice. (London: Sage Publications, 2000), 4. This kind of teaching only serves to reproduce the inequitable power relations between different classes in a society and becomes complicit in the social violence inherent in that systematic inequity. Education, in short, becomes primarily the property of the privileged wielded for the ongoing maintenance of that privilege.

students or professors from the dominant culture were to preach in the minority student's home church they would only be politely endured. The same can happen in the pastoral staff meeting of a diverse church after a staff member preaches. The staff member's preaching communicated "you can trust me" to a sector of the church the lead pastor may not typically reach in the same way. If the lead pastor is not careful, she may critique the preaching for the very things that made it valuable to the broader mission of the church.

This does not mean that class-related signals are above critique. Instead, the above reminds preachers and professors of the need to engage in descriptive feedback so that ministers might be prompted toward theological critique of cultural norms from the inside. To give good feedback we often need to *simply describe what happened* as clearly as a mirror describes our own appearance to us. In preaching as in life, a revealing mirror is a painful but helpful component of self-awareness. In this way, neither the insider nor the outsider is silenced and what is seen as "inside" and what is "outside" often change places.

The middle-class preacher admits that the lower-class experience is outside of his zone of experience and confidence. The white preacher admits that minorities might not resonate with the ways of preaching she has come to believe are the standard. Classes and cultures of privilege and power may be blinded to critique from within requiring a critique from the margins funded by the grace of the gospel. Valuing diversity in preaching requires more than a surface commitment to inclusion. Deeply held values about what is good and bad often have to be changed and recognized as more limited than we believe. Part of what makes preaching "good" in the ears and eyes of the congregant is the preacher's ability to speak from a settled identity that is contextually shaped, while speaking across cultures and contexts with sincerity and skill.

All of the above discussion of culturally formed ways of being provides a problem for the "virtues." MacIntyre appears to describe them a-contextually, as if context were irrelevant. How can virtues be defined for a diverse set of preachers for whom context matters deeply in the way they show virtue? Because of the need to speak both to and across diverse contexts, the virtues for preaching are defined in great degree by responsiveness to context. This great weakness of MacIntyre, as well as many discussions of virtue, is gravely important for preaching. *There is no such thing as context-free virtue.* When an ox is in the ditch on the Sabbath, the context matters. When a Samaritan woman is alone at the well, context matters. Context always matters.

There are, therefore, virtues requisite to the practice of preaching that do cross over boundaries of context and class (MacIntyre's point) even if their expression is contextual (Bourdieu's argument). Both poles are held together in what I call contextual virtues. *Contextual virtues* are good precisely in and because of their loving attendance to contextual and cultural concerns. They are the various contextual forms love takes as it actively engages practices and the people who participate in them. These *contextual virtues* need to be formed in all preachers if they are to direct preaching toward its aim, facilitate its functions, and wisely balance the enjoyment of internal and external goods. Homiletics must discern which elements of so-called good preaching are signs of context-specific dispositions (instead of forcing a particular class *habitus*) and which indicate *contextual virtues* of the formative practice that cross over from one context to the next. The former, uncovering context-specific signals of common values, is a never-ending task *on the job* that should be guided by the contextual virtues of preaching.[22]

This summary analysis of practices in general leaves the reader with specific pressing questions to ask of the practice of preaching. What is the aim of preaching? This should shape the preacher's *longing*. What are the central functions the practice of preaching is especially fitted to accomplish? The functions shape the preacher's *doing*. What contextual virtues support the aim, facilitate the functions, and enable the judicious balance of internal and external goods? The contextual virtues shape the preacher's way of *being*.

For Reflection

1. Spend some time reflecting on or discussing the internal goods and external goods of preaching. This chapter gives some of

---

22. Identifying and defining the contextual virtues is the ultimate aim of chapter 3.

the more obvious examples. What other internal and external goods exist for the practice of preaching?

2. What are some of the culturally formed ways of being (*habitus*) with which congregations in your home context automatically resonate? What is it preachers do to signal "I understand you" or even "I am like you in this way" to the community?

3. What are some culturally formed ways of being (*habitus*) that preachers have used in your home context that showed they were strange to the context or not aware of the communal norms?

4. Is there an unconscious or conscious habit given to you by your original community that might be harming your preaching as you move into other diverse contexts or try to reach a more diverse congregation in your home context?

5. Have you received a critique of your preaching you now recognize to be culturally or contextually bound? In what contexts would that feedback be most helpful? In what contexts should you maintain your former practice?

CHAPTER 2
What Preaching Does Best

When someone finally discerns what she does best, that person usually uncovers her own truest longing. Until then we are often Martha, worried and distracted by many things. When a minister focuses her life according to a true and deep longing, it is hard to overestimate how much good she can accomplish. Preaching is often like the gifted minister. Preaching has too many possibilities to pursue, too many requests and aims from outsiders. If preaching is pressed to do everything it can do, it will crumple under the weight of seeking to please too many masters. In order to define and limit the expectations on preachers and preaching, this chapter will explore the preacher's longing and define the preacher's doing. The next chapter will sketch the preacher's way of being.

The good preacher's longing is shaped by the aim of preaching. The good preacher's doing is guided by the functions of preaching. The good preacher's being is characterized by the contextual virtues of preaching. The preacher's longing, doing, and being are what make a preacher truly good. When these are out of order, even though preaching skills are in place, a preacher is not truly good even if he is excellent. When a preacher is short on preaching skills, but these things are in order, they may be truly called "good" in the most important sense of the term. Great preachers are both good and excellent at the same time.

It is not our doing that first drives us toward better preaching. It is our longing. A misdirected longing is like a dog left alone who eagerly devours a neglected candy bar. The misdirected longing brings short-term pleasure and long-term misery. For many preachers do not realize the misery they experience is the result of their longing. If a preacher misunderstands what preaching does best, that preacher may miss the beauty of the preaching life. Burnout, compassion fatigue, and perfectionism among other things can consume the preacher's joy. Our task in this chapter is to consider the historic wisdom regarding what preaching does best. When preachers recognize what preaching does best and how it does it best, they can reorient their longings for preaching accordingly.

Preachers do long for many things. If it is Monday, you might be yearning for a few Sundays off. If it is Thursday, perhaps you long for just one more sermon to finally come together—just one more, Lord. Sunday afternoon, all you can think of desiring is a nap. These short-term desires are not the longing this chapter addresses. What does a preacher *as a preacher* long to have happen through preaching? A preacher may fantasize about glory or fame in the Christian celebrity world. A preacher may even fantasize about the perfect sermon like a holy grail of sermonic work. A preacher may desire immediate, universal, and enthusiastic celebration of his sermons. These flights of fancy are not the deepest longings of our best selves. They are normal, human, and often harmful if nurtured.

Christians do not think first of their longings and then direct their lives accordingly. Instead Christians seek to direct their lives rightly and align their longings accordingly. We have a larger aim than happiness in the moment; we seek unending joy. The heart is deceitful above all things, the prophet warns us. It will misguide and misdirect us one day and steer us with a righteous precision the next. When we follow our short-term desires and fantasies we end up with lives filled with heartache, disappointment, and regrettable mistakes. Perhaps it will help to begin our exploration of the preacher's longing by listing desires that might mislead us into thinking they are the aim of preaching.

The aim of preaching is not a good sermon.

The aim of preaching is not a successful ministry.

The aim of preaching is not the respect of our community or peers.

The aim of preaching is not the chance to preach in more prestigious places.

The aim of preaching is not to be perceived as spiritual or holy.

The aim of preaching is not to save souls.

The aim of preaching is not to teach doctrine.

The aim of preaching is not to heal hearts.

The aim of preaching is not to undo unjust wrongs.

The aim of preaching is not to tear down oppressive structures.

Certainly, some of the above are greater and nobler than others, but all fall short of the glory of what preaching has aimed for across the ages. All of these things are too small for preaching and too short a vision for the preacher's heart. Each of these desires, even the ones that are twisted toward selfish ends, has something to do with the aim of preaching but is not the aim itself. If we want to practice the preaching life we must aim that life in the right direction and order our longings according to our aim. Preachers need to aim at the right end and hope to achieve it.

The Preacher's Longing: Drawn to the Aim of Preaching

How can we discern a better aim for preaching than the ones above? There is general agreement among practice theorists at large,[1] and practice-oriented homileticians in specific,[2] that a practice is always rooted historically and carries with it a wisdom bound up in its tradition. This being the

---

1. For an exploration of twentieth-century philosophy from the standpoint of practices, see Stanley P. Turner, *The Social Theory of Practices: Tradition, Tacit Knowledge, and Presuppositions* (Chicago: University of Chicago Press, 1994). For discussions of tradition and practice, especially note pp. 94–99.

2. Such as Charles Campbell, James Nieman, Leonora Tubbs Tisdale, and Thomas Long among others. See Charles L. Campbell, *The Word before the Powers: An Ethic of Preaching*, 1st ed. (Louisville, KY: Westminster John Knox Press, 2002) and Thomas G. Long and Leonora Tubbs Tisdale, eds., *Teaching Preaching as a Christian Practice: A New Approach to Homiletical Pedagogy*, 1st ed. (Louisville, KY: Westminster John Knox Press, 2008).

case, the obvious questions for a practice-focused view of preaching are: How does one gain initial access to this tradition? Where does one start?

Augustine of Hippo's *De doctrina christiana* (*On Christian Teaching*) has been dubbed "the jewel of Christian works on preaching" and was considered the foremost word on preaching for Christianity for more than one thousand years.[3] St. Augustine began writing this work around AD 397, took a break from the work during the heavier seasons of his ministry and doctrinal battles, and validated his earlier writing by finishing the work in AD 427. Until the 1500s this book dominated preaching. *On Christian Teaching* is still required reading for many theological schools and seminaries around the world. As such it is not an exaggeration to say that this is the earliest and most influential preaching textbook of all time. Because of this Augustine is the starting point for historic exploration of the preacher's longing, doing, and being. Yet Augustine did not pen the conclusion on these things. Much has been learned and added to our understanding of preaching that should not be ignored.

Early in his writing in *On Christian Teaching* Augustine makes it clear that good preaching is ultimately directed toward the same aim as all activity: the enjoyment of God. This aim is not merely a Christian truism for Augustine, however. To explain this purpose, he engages in an extended and complicated discussion of hermeneutics following a two fold division of reality into signs and things. To Augustine the way we understand reality is structured according to the double love command. The ultimate aim of all is to promote the love of God and neighbor.[4] This is not a discussion of philosophy or hermeneutics in the abstract. Augustine wants to explore the "sort of person those who seek" to teach and preach "ought to be."[5] For

---

3. John J. Gavigan, "Augustine's Use of the Classics," *The Classical Weekly* 39, no. 7 (1945): 50–53. See also Thomas Conley, *Rhetoric in the European Tradition* (Chicago: University of Chicago Press, 1990), 82.

4. For a charitable reading of Augustine's injunction to "use" the neighbor in a noninstrumental sense, see especially Helmut David Baer, "The Fruit of Charity: Using the Neighbor in 'De Doctrina Christiana,'" *Journal of Religious Ethics* 24, no. 1 (Spring 1996): 47–64.

5. Augustine, *On Christian Teaching*, trans. R. P. H. Green (New York: Oxford University Press, 1997), 146 (4.31.64). I am including the most common (though not most recent) numbering system for *De doctrina christiana* in the Latin text in parentheses as well as the citation for the English text, translated by R. P. H. Green, unless otherwise noted. Other English translations consulted include *St. Augustine's On Christian Doctrine*, trans. J. F. Shaw, Nicene and Post-Nicene Fathers, 1st ser., vol. 2 (Grand Rapids, MI: William B. Eerdmans, 1979).

Augustine, his discussion of the enjoyment of God, signs and things, love of neighbor, and so forth is all intended to help the preacher and teacher become a good preacher, a good teacher.

A *doxological* aim for preaching derives most naturally and directly from the overall aim of life for Augustine: to love and enjoy God. Maintaining Augustine's interpretive lens, the double love command, he requires that preaching be a means for the love and enjoyment of God and the love of neighbor motivated by the love of God. Preaching is first and foremost, for preacher and community, a doxological activity. From this perspective, preaching is an act of worship that is necessarily performative, not an act of performance that just so happens to be in a setting of worship. The performative and rhetorical aspects of preaching find their proper place in an attitude of worship. Preaching is a human act offered in service of a worshipful life. Preaching seeks to shape a doxological or a worshipping community that is honoring to God.

When preachers squint questioningly at the performance components of preaching, it is usually out of one of two fears. One fear is the diminishment of preaching's focus on its defining context: worship. We fear that when preachers knowingly perform, they seek to gain approval of humans, not ascribe glory and worth to God. The other fear is the confusion of means with end. Performance is a means not an end. This priority of order transforms the preacher's relationship to performance deeply at the level of strategic concern. When priority is placed on doxology, it necessarily focuses the preacher's strategic concern on the internal good of worshipping God. This naturally emphasizes the real person of the preacher as that preacher *is* in the moment of preaching. Preaching is certainly not worshipful if it is a knowingly and capriciously sloppy performance. Yet, when a life of worship in community is the ultimate aim, the driving motivation of the preacher is a loving enjoyment of God (a desire to make a good offering), not a fearful pleasing of neighbor (performance anxiety).

This priority on doxology also helps avoid two forms of homiletical "heresy." Homiletical Donatism and homiletical Docetism are two poles of misguided attitude toward preaching.[6] Homiletical Donatism overemphasizes the person of the preacher and the embodiment of the sermon to the point of moralism or perfectionism. This Donatistic view of preaching leads the preacher to think that his own lack of righteousness or poor performance renders his preaching unusable by God, or the reverse. A doxological focus emphasizes the person that the preacher actually *is in the moment* of preaching and the attitude in that moment. Doxological preaching gives performative elements of preaching a new master and a new end: worshipful enjoyment of God through preaching, even in the preaching moment.

Docetism in preaching form makes the human portions of preaching only seem to matter. The preacher prays Docetic prayers such as "Let them see you, not me. Hide me behind the cross."[7] A preacher who wishes only to *appear* to be present while preaching is deluding herself. The preacher may also be tempted to think that his abusive behavior, or his lack of performative effort, has no bearing on preaching's effects. Worship is not dependent on moral perfection, yet it does require the engagement of the actual person. Worship is not primarily performance, yet there is always a performative element. To disregard the performative element is to bring a poor offering, to walk away with Cain's downcast face.

The desire of the preacher to *enjoy the giving of a good offering* steers between the shoals of moralism and amorality, perfectionism and sloth. A sermon deeply internalized, well embodied, and lovingly delivered is like the singing of a favorite worship song full-throated. In other words, preaching can and should be both fun and good at the same time because preaching is an activity of worship aimed at forming a community in a life of worship. When all is going well, the joy of preaching is worth the sacrifice a good offering requires.

---

6. André Resner, *Preacher and Cross: Person and Message in Theology and Rhetoric* (Grand Rapids, MI: William B. Eerdmans, 1999), 62ff. Resner modifies the conceptions of heresies as a homiletical way of thought from the concepts worded differently in Clyde E. Fant, *Preaching for Today*, 1st ed. (New York: Harper & Row, 1975).

7. The Greek word *dokeo* means "to appear or seem." Docetics longed to elevate the divinity of Christ and feared humanity sullied the Godhead. Therefore, Christ only appeared to be human, only appeared to have flesh and bone.

I teach preachers in undergraduate-, masters-, and doctoral-level education. In each of these levels there is always a student who is not sure that preaching is his or her "thing." One of the joys of teaching preaching for me is the journey these students often take from viewing preaching as an unbearable burden or an unreachable skill toward viewing preaching as an act of worship they can deeply enjoy. I often tell the preacher in a quiet prayer moment in the hall before the preaching class begins, "You've done the work. Now let go and have fun. Enjoy preaching this like you would enjoy singing your favorite worship song. Get into the rhythm of it and let it sing from your heart." I watch as the furrowed brow flattens, the jaw relaxes, the lips turn into a smile, and the light returns to the eyes. Remembering preaching is an act of worship is like being surprised by an old friend in a crowded airport. The layover is transformed from stress to laughter, from endurance to enjoyment, from too long of a wait before the next thing to too short a time to enjoy life together.

It would be misleading to limit Augustine's thoughts on the doxological nature of preaching to the preacher alone. Clearly Augustine aims at the formation of an entire community whose whole life is worshipful in its orientation. Further, Augustine does not limit these thoughts to the four walls of a local worshipping community. His discussion of compassion for neighbor and his extension of that compassion to all potential neighbors indicate Augustine's desire for the church to exist for the sake of the world. Preaching is a communal practice that requires both preacher and congregation, is for the church only insofar as the church is for the world, and seeks to launch that church into a worshipful form of life in the world. Further, Augustine indicates throughout the work that the proclamation of the gospel (*praedicandi evangelii*) is a key portion of the aim of the preacher.

A thorough examination of the history of homiletics to demonstrate the consistency with which these categories reemerge under different form is beyond the scope of this book. It is also likely unnecessary. The claims above "ring true" with preachers from many theological traditions, social locations, and cultural backgrounds. In southern or northern latitudes, eastern or western longitudes, in places of plenty and conditions of need,

I have seen this view of preaching resonate deeply with pastors around the world. Mainline, Evangelical, Pentecostal, and Catholic preachers have all given a resounding *amen* when they hear these thoughts. When we gather all of the above thoughts together, here is one way to express the aim of preaching, which shapes the longing of the preacher:

Preaching aims to send a doxological community into the world through the proclamation of the gospel.

This is the aim of preaching under which all visions of the preacher (shepherd, herald, witness, prophet, priest, and more) find a unified home. This is the aim of preaching under which all the types of preaching find a unified home. From didactic to catechetical, from festal to evangelistic preaching, from expositional to topical, from deductive to inductive, all good preaching seeks to send a doxological community into the world through the proclamation of the gospel.[8]

Because of this aim, several characteristics of the preaching practice already begin to emerge. Since preaching aims at sending a doxological community, its tones and modes are akin to the tones and modes of worship: lament, celebration, praise, plea, and more. Because preaching aims at communal life, it is best pursued and practiced communally not individually. Since preaching intends to *send* that worshipful community, it must always maintain an outward focus.

Certain forms of theology emphasize individual portions of the statement more than others. Missional theology, for example, emphasizes heavily the sent nature of the community and the sending nature of preaching. Neoorthodox theology has typically emphasized more heavily the proclamatory nature of preaching with a strong view of the agency of God's "voice" through human words. In Anglican and Episcopal traditions it could be argued that the doxological function of all practices, not only preaching, has been emphasized more heavily. In post-liberal theology it is the communal nature of the aim that will probably grab the attention

---

8. Hughes Oliphant Old offers us many of these categories in his magisterial work on the history of preaching, *The Reading and Preaching of the Scriptures in the Worship of the Christian Church*, 7 vols. (Grand Rapids, MI: William B. Eerdmans, 1998).

of the reader. A celebration of the community, communal interpretation, communal life, and a communally shared grand story saturates post-liberal thought. In Evangelical traditions, the word *gospel* is what will likely resonate deeply and its sending nature assumed. In Lutheran traditions, the word *gospel* will also ring true but bear a different meaning. Doxology as love of neighbor will be the rhythm particular traditions beat with passion until the preaching drum of justice nearly breaks. As with any family squabble, each party has a sector of truth, and each has a very difficult time recognizing the other's contribution.

Once the above aim for preaching is fully in view and deeply understood, the squabbles seem to be more clearly understood, at least for preaching, as differences of emphases not differences of aim. The theological and philosophical disagreements run deep to be sure, but the overarching aim allows room for those differences to remain in community formed by a larger agreement. There is a very good reason why preachers who could not ascribe to the same ecclesial structures historically have found ways to preach next to one another out of unity of aim.[9]

This aim also allows for us to have more clear-headed examination of popular Christian culture's means of measuring how well preaching is going. When preaching does its part in growing a church, it may or may not help to accomplish the aim of preaching. It depends on the kind of church community that surrounds it, the movement of that church in relation to the world, and the tone of the communal life. When preaching reaches the typical standards of excellence rhetorically, performatively, and even doctrinally it may or may not be doing its part in achieving the aim. After all, some of the most magnificent performances of sermons, the most persuasive of Christian speeches, the most doctrinally pure messages have fallen short of sending a worshipful community into the world for the sake of that world. The preacher had a different aim in view.

When preaching does not send a doxological community into the world, does that mean it has failed to seek its aim? Not necessarily. Time is littered with the unfulfilled lives of faithful and good people. Christian

---

9. Consider the Wesleyan revival in England, or the civil rights movement in North America for strong examples.

history rarely mentions those who did everything right but were ignored by their communities, even expelled by the official church. They fought the good fight quietly in forgotten corners where only the God who sees what is done in secret would remember. This said, a church or ministry must ask difficult questions of itself if some portion of that aim is not being achieved in demonstrable ways through its preaching and other practices.

If preaching sends a doxological community into the world, but not through the proclamation of the gospel, has it failed to seek its aim? Most certainly it has. This does not imply a narrow or parochial view of what the gospel is. However, if preaching cannot discernibly articulate the good news, if preaching is received primarily as bad news, if preaching offers good platitudes that are hardly news, if preaching follows the psychological or philosophical winds of time without offering a word that breaks in from the outside, if preaching is moralistic or legalistic rather than good news, then preaching has not fully sought its aim. Preaching may "do good" without a gospel, but it does not do what preaching does *best*. Gospel-less preaching plays a field others play just as well or better.

The outward moving and returning church, the giving and sacrificial church, the forgiving and accepting church, the missional and liberating church, the healing and whole church is the *amen* to the preaching of the church. No lesser *amen* will fully satisfy. This is another way of saying that the preacher is not the only contributor to the practice of preaching. The listeners who form the congregation of the day either help to complete the sermon by accepting it and enacting it in their lives, or help to thwart the sermon by doing anything less.[10] The practice of preaching belongs to the whole church; it is not the sole province of the preacher.

Given the above aim for the practice of preaching, the longing of the preacher needs to be realigned with the aim. If the longing of the preacher is directed toward any lesser desire, a turning of the heart is necessary. When the preacher's heart is aligned with the aim of preaching,

---

10. It is worth mentioning that at times the congregation resists preaching for good reason. When this is the case, we rejoice that a sermon is allowed to die in the quickly thinning air just after the final benediction. Every experienced preacher has a few sermons she laid to rest with only minor movements of grief.

the longing of the preacher transcends the desire for a single good sermon. The longing of the preacher is for the just and righteous reign of God to move forward in the world so every neighbor is loved in tangible and equitable ways. The longing of the preacher is for the people of God to enjoy a worshipful life in the world. The longing of the preacher is for the community of the people of God to be united in the worship of God in the world. The longing of the preacher is for the community of the people of God to bring benefit to the reputation of God so the greater church is perceived as a gift and not a burden to the world, a bringer of peace, a harbinger of justice, a living parable of all that is right and good and true.

Therefore, the longing of the preacher is to gather, but also to send; not merely to teach, but to deeply disciple; not only to heal souls, but to commission the church as a healing force for peace; not merely to delight the listener, but to move a worshipping community out into the world. The glory-seeking preacher is not shamed here but swept up into a vision of glory giving. The perfectionist preacher is not condemned here but given a higher end to pursue than the flawless sermon. The artistic wordsmith is not told to set aside the linguistic hammer and tongs but invited to employ the same tools to more glorious ends.

The Preacher's Doing: The Functions of Good Preaching

It seems simplistic at first to ask what a preacher does. After all, preachers simply preach. They discover, develop, and embody sermons. What else is there? The answer only raises other questions. What is a sermon, and what does a sermon do? More to the point, even though a single sermon cannot do too many things all at once, the practice of preaching does much more than any single sermon could accomplish alone. The sermon this week may do something very different from what the sermon does next week. Preachers need to pay attention to this fact. Shortsighted focus on one sermon at a time will miss the most powerful potential for preaching: its repeated, over-time, and holistically shaping force.

We begin our search for preaching's functions in the same place that we began our search for preaching's aim, in the most influential preaching textbook in history. The ensuing history of preaching and preaching theory will fill in the gaps many discern in Augustine. Though Augustine does not use the precise language of function, his assumed functions for preaching become clear with a close reading. The first function of preaching for Augustine is a therapeutic one: healing.

Therapeutic preaching has become a loaded phrase in homiletics since the mid- to late twentieth century.[11] Therapeutic preaching is now decried as trivializing the gospel or diminishing God to a reverse projection of our human needs. God is a nice God who wants us all to be nice and who is there for us if we ever have need.[12] These concerns are valid and crucial today. Yet for Augustine, none of the baggage of cheap pop psychology with which Western culture now has to deal weighs him down. Neither does highly anthropological nineteenth-century liberalism concern him. To be sure, his God was not reduced to a loving parental figure asking us to be nice. Though I must admit, being nice would be a good step toward love for some people of faith. Rather, medicinal metaphors seemed particularly appropriate to him given the healing metaphors used throughout Scripture.

For Augustine, the healing function of preaching emerges from the activity of God. Augustine therefore explores how the Wisdom of God healed humanity by coming in the flesh.[13] God accomplished this healing by first of all being sufferer, medicine, and physician in the same person. Jesus Christ is both the balm and the hand applying the balm with full

---

11. See Kenda Creasy Dean's helpful analysis of survey findings on adolescent faith in *Almost Christian: What the Faith of Our Teenagers Is Telling the American Church* (Oxford: Oxford University Press, 2010). Her study offers insight for preaching to youth and young adults from Christian Smith and Melina Lundquist Denton's research in *Soul Searching: The Religious and Spiritual Lives of American Teenagers* (Oxford: Oxford University Press, 2009). It should be mentioned that the youth of this study are now adults at the time of this writing. There is no empirical evidence or logical reason to assume their faith is substantively different simply by the passing of more years under the moral therapeutic deism of the preaching and teaching of the church culture that raised them.

12. For an insightful critique of therapeutic preaching in the twentieth-century sense, see David Buttrick's "A Fearful Pulpit, a Wayward Land" in *What's the Matter with Preaching Today*, ed. Mike Graves (Louisville, KY: Westminster John Knox Press, 2004), esp. 40–42.

13. Augustine, *De doctrina christiana*, 1.13.12 through 1.25.15.

empathy since he suffered the sickness we have suffered: human frailty in all its forms. Second, the triune God accomplished this healing by fitting the cure to the wound "curing some of them by their likes, some of them by their opposites."[14] Augustine in this section is laying theological groundwork for human care and skill in teaching and preaching Christian doctrine. As a good doctor educates a patient, so this therapeutic function blends into the didactic. *Preaching functions therapeutically by attending to the needs and hurts of fallen humanity in order to meet needs and heal wounds with the proclamation of the gospel.* In this way preaching *heals*. Insofar as many Christian contexts around the world continue to report physical healing following on the heels of preaching and teaching faith, it must be mentioned that perhaps preaching pays an occasional and unpredictable healing role in even more literal ways.[15]

The second function of preaching discernible in Augustine is the didactic function: teaching.[16] The title of the text *De doctrina christiana* clearly indicates Augustine's view of preaching and teaching. Teaching and preaching in Christian contexts are inextricably interwoven. Above all else, as will be explored below, the Christian orator is to be clear, to be easily understood, and to promote the teaching of the rule of faith as expressed in the whole panoply of scripture.[17] *Preaching is didactic, a process of educating the nonbeliever, the immature believer, and the mature believer in those elements of Christian doctrine that are most appropriate to their ongoing pilgrimage toward God.*

When I offer these thoughts in preaching courses and conferences there is occasional resistance to the idea of preaching as teaching. For some, this comes from exegetical decisions that divide two words in

---

14. Augustine, *On Christian Doctrine*, trans. D. W. Robertson Jr. (Indianapolis, IN: Hayes Barton Press, 1965), 9–10.

15. My friends in India, Indonesia, the Philippines, Haiti, Nigeria, Nepal, and other locations indicate the opposite of typical Western Christian views of healing. According to them, many local communities consider a pastor who has not seen healing appear through his or her ministry an imposter. Westerners often celebrate diversity verbally but reject diverse perspectives such as these.

16. For a description of catechetical preaching as a type of preaching that teaches throughout Christian history, see Hughes Oliphant Old, *The Reading and Preaching of the Scriptures in the Worship of the Christian Church:* vol. 5, *The Biblical Period* (Grand Rapids, MI: William B. Eerdmans, 1998), 13–16. The teaching function of preaching is a much larger category that subsumes the catechetical type described by Old.

17. Augustine, *De doctrina christiana*, 4.8.22.

scripture that most often show up together, *preaching* and *teaching*.[18] For others, the division is a protection of the turf of Christian education and spiritual formation. Christian education teaches after all. The early Christians did not divide so neatly between preaching and teaching as we do. Upon reflection you might find that most of your favorite teachers and preachers have moved fluidly back and forth between those two. When speaking of God, it is a timid teacher who never proclaims and a shallow preacher who has nothing to teach. For preaching, teaching is only one function. For Christian education, it is certainly a central one.

Third, preaching performs a soteriological function: saving.[19] Augustine not only connects the incarnation in general with preaching in general but also quotes 1 Corinthians 1:21 to give a soteriological function in specific to his particularly incarnational theology of preaching: "to save those that believe through the foolishness of preaching."[20] The embodiment of the gospel in the person of the preacher, no matter how ridiculous it may seem, *to redeem and reconcile the listener to God.*

Augustine follows the Johannine description of eternal life beginning with the love of God and neighbor in temporal life. This *is* eternal life. Preaching saves humanity from the love of things, which are to be used, and the use of that which is to be enjoyed. Preaching saves humanity from the love of false gods masquerading as ultimate ends. Preaching instructs, delights, and moves humanity toward the ethical love of neighbor as anyone "to whom an act of compassion is due" and "who can fail to see that there is no exception to this, nobody to whom compassion is not due?"[21]

---

18. Scriptural authors often use variations of *didasko* and *euangelizo. Parakaleo, kerusso,* and *katangello* are also used where preaching is the translation (pointing to the multiple functions and tones of the practice of preaching). For examples of the connection, see the narrative of Jesus's teaching in the synagogue in Luke 4, in which proclamation is his central purpose. See also Acts 15:35 and 28:31, though examples abound.

19. Here Augustine is usually thought to be in line with what Old titles "Evangelistic preaching" in *Reading and Preaching of the Scriptures: The Biblical Period* (pp. 9–13). However, salvation for Augustine is not merely conversion but formation or salvation from "perverse contracts," bad habits, and evil character (Augustine, *On Christian Teaching,* 19). As a result, he may be more in line with the view of preaching David Buttrick outlines in *Homiletic: Moves and Structures,* in which the church through preaching is understood as the "ones being saved in the world" (Philadelphia: Fortress Press, 1988), 41. Buttrick's understanding of salvation is not merely eschatological in scope and neither is Augustine's.

20. Augustine, *On Christian Teaching,* 13 (1.12.12).

21. Ibid., 23 (1.30.31).

Augustine builds this argument on Paul's summation of the Ten Commandments into the love of neighbor in Romans 13:9-10. As a result, he can state:

> Anyone who thinks that the apostle was not here giving commandments to all people is compelled to admit something totally absurd and wicked: that Paul thought it no sin to violate the wife of a non-Christian or an enemy, or to kill him or covet his property. If this conclusion is absurd (*dimentis*), it is clear that all people must be reckoned as neighbors, because evil must not be done to anyone.[22]

For Augustine, then, the practice of preaching exists for the sake of fulfilling the double law of love using the proclamation of the gospel to worship God with the hope of healing hearts, teaching minds, and saving souls from idolatrous attachment. Augustine claims that doxology is the key in which the song of preaching is always sung. The hope of the preacher is that others might begin to sing their own lives in the same worshipful key. To aid this transposition from idolatry to doxology in neighbor as well as herself the preacher seeks to heal, to teach, and to save using words that remain inadequate to these tasks but with faith that God promises to infuse these with grace.

St. Augustine, the bishop of Hippo, wrote from a place of undeniable privilege and power. Though his preaching often spoke of the need to love and tangibly serve the poor, the outcast, and the downtrodden, this makes many suspicious of his ability to see clearly the gospel that was always particularly to and for the poor. The critique is that though Augustine was aware of the scriptural call to take care of the poor and to seek justice in an unjust society, those issues never operated in the forefront of his mind in his theological constructs. Though these critiques are at times too extreme, they are not wrong. Unless one assumes that Augustine subsumes the poor and outcast underneath the functions of teaching, healing, and saving it is a relatively absent concern for his preaching theory. As a result it is necessary to learn from the remainder of homiletical history something

---

22. Ibid., 23 (1.30.31–32). Parenthetical Latin is added.

that is missing in the functions of preaching if healing, teaching, and saving are all that is envisioned.

At the end of Augustine's posthumous reign as preaching professor supreme the mendicant friars of St. Francis of Assisi are perhaps the first and strongest voice to make justice in service to the poor a central concern of Christian preaching. This concern is not as dominant in the reflections on preaching reformers such as Martin Luther or John Calvin give.[23] Neither does it find a foothold in the extravagant rhetorical flourish of the French or continental preachers in the 1600s until the revival of concern for the poor emerged in preachers such as Bossuet.[24] In the 1700s, preachers such as John and Charles Wesley, George Whitfield, and other like-minded ministers pressed regularly for a concern for the poor and the oppressed of society.[25] In the 1800s, abolitionist movements in Europe and the Americas conceived of preaching as a vehicle for the liberation of the oppressed.[26] Homiletic theorists of the late twentieth century and early twenty-first century have consistently highlighted the need for the proclamation of mercy and justice from the pulpit.[27] As a result we need to add to the three functions of preaching a liberating fourth: freeing.

23. In spite of a lesser focus on justice in direct reflections on preaching in Luther and Calvin's writings, it is clear their preaching acted to liberate oppressed persons, pressing for justice with incredible courage. Both Luther and Calvin were outcasts and ecclesial/political refugees. Indulgences were likely opposed primarily because of the gross injustice of the practice, not only the theological absurdity. Calvin's preaching has been recently highlighted as unflinchingly focused on justice when the exposition of the text led him to do so. See Andrew Thompson Scales, "Justice and Equity: Calvin's 1550 Sermon on Micah 2:1" (paper presented to the History of Homiletics Workgroup, Academy of Homiletics, Dallas, TX, December 2017).

24. Jacques B. Bossuet, "On the Eminent Dignity of the Poor in the Church: A Sermon by Jacques Bénigne Bossuet," trans. Edward R. Udovic, *Vincentian Heritage Journal* 13, no. 1 (1992): 37–58.

25. Old calls John Wesley the "Protestant Francis of Assisi" in *Reading and Preaching of the Scriptures*, 5: 111.

26. An accessible introduction into some of the unexpected sources of fervor for justice and mercy is found in the revised version of Donald Dayton's classic work *Rediscovering an Evangelical Heritage: A Tradition and Trajectory of Integrating Piety and Justice* (Grand Rapids, MI: Baker Academic, 2014). Here the Evangelical roots in justice-focused ministries are made clear. This makes the labeling of "Evangelicals" in current discussions troublingly two dimensional, defining Evangelicals by their least desirable parties.

27. For a beginning orientation to the numerous works that inform this conclusion, see the following: Walter Brueggemann, *The Practice of Prophetic Imagination: Preaching an Emancipating Word* (Minneapolis: Fortress Press, 2012); Kenyatta R. Gilbert, *The Journey and Promise of African American Preaching* (Minneapolis: Fortress Press, 2011); Leonora Tubbs Tisdale, *Prophetic Preaching: A Pastoral Approach* (Louisville, KY: Westminster John Knox Press, 2010); J. Philip Wogaman, *Speaking the Truth in Love: Prophetic Preaching to a Broken World* (Louisville, KY: Westminster John Knox Press, 1998).

The functions of preaching do not live in the cages of these categories. Though a single good sermon might be primarily didactic, it most likely has at least traces of one or more of the other functions as well. The following diagram may help to visualize the relationships between the aim of preaching and its four functions.

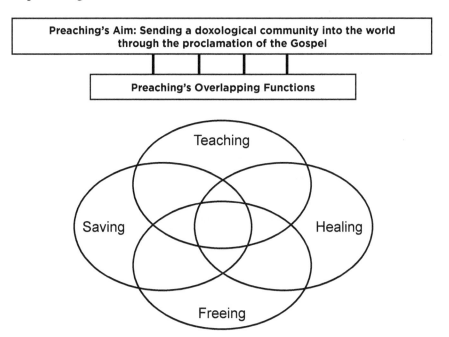

This graphic serves to illustrate several key concepts related to the functions of preaching before moving on. First, the functions of preaching are better understood as overlapping zones or modes rather than discrete cages of function or content. A single sermon may serve two functions well, but rarely will every sermon emphasize all four. A sermon that functions primarily to teach should be careful to at least consider the other functions to be sure it is not weakened by their absence. Many sermons lack primarily a sentence or two, here and there, as a tip of the hat to the other functions of preaching. Just a sentence allows the listener to wait for another day for what their heart is longing to hear more deeply.

Second, the whole picture of preaching requires attendance over time to these four functions. A preaching ministry that avoids teaching for fear of boring the listener has slipped into entertainment-minded modes. A preaching ministry that across time avoids the liberating function of the gospel for political or pragmatic fears may need to call into question the validity of the other functions as well. Though a particular preacher on a particular day cannot be expected to achieve all of these functions, the practice of preaching in a community of faith across time can be. Wise ministers will insist preaching do so.

Other Christian practices teach, heal, save, or free. So how is it true that these are what preaching does best? It is also true other Christian practices seek to send a doxological community into the world. It is the end phrase of the aim of preaching that clarifies *how* preaching does these things best. It is through the proclamation of the gospel. The overarching aim of the practice of preaching must interface with the overarching aim of worship or Christian education to be sure. And no practice is the only practice that accomplishes what that practice accomplishes. Yet every practice accomplishes what it accomplishes, and aims for what it aims for in its own unique way. The way of preaching is the proclamation of the good news.

Even when the attempt to send is met with resistance and apathy, when the community is not accepting, when the worship of the preacher is not matched with the worship of the people or vice versa, if the gospel has been proclaimed, then there is reason to celebrate. Proclamation of the gospel then is not only a means to the end but also a part of the end itself. Proclamation of the gospel is not only part of the aim as a primary means but also the defining characteristic of each of the functions. The good news is what is taught; the good news is what rescues; the good news is what heals; and the good news is what sets us free. If the good news only saves us in a limited sense, then our good news is too small. Often a key critique of a preaching practice over time is not that there is no gospel but that the gospel is too narrow. The domesticated or radicalized, otherworldly or humanistic, shallow or intellectualized gospels are all only partial gospels.

What does preaching do best? Preaching sends a doxological community into the world by proclaiming the gospel in ways that teach, heal, save, and free. No single sermon can encompass all of this. For that matter, preaching does not seek to fully accomplish its own game on its own power. The practice of preaching regularly teaches us to engage other Christian practices. The practice of preaching regularly gives us the medicine that heals our soul *through* other Christian practices. The practice of preaching saves us from addictive attachments and replaces them with Christian practices. The practice of preaching prompts people to engage in things such as hospitality, generous giving, face-to-face relationship, reconciliation, peacemaking, and more in order to truly send a doxological community into the world funded by the gospel.

When I think of the aim and functions of preaching I am most often reminded of preaching movements in places other than the culture and nation where I live. The bi-vocational pastors in impoverished communities who give up pay in order to have a week of learning to preach and teach better inspire me. They do not make a virtue of necessity, asking all other pastors to be bi-vocational. Neither do they give up virtue because of difficulty. The pastors who wade through waist-high waters in typhoons to have a chance to share the good news that has transformed their hearts encourage me. More than the individuals it is the fact that the worshipful missional energy is what characterizes the community of pastors and congregations of which they are a part. They worship in simple church buildings, turning people away for the sake of fire code. These preachers invite those waiting to get in to the next service. There are open-air worship spaces where people gather not just weekly but often nightly in the equatorial heat for singing, praying, and preaching. These are communities of worship who are the greatest source of belonging, hope, food, and clothing, and they are the best network for employment and opportunity people can find. They do not just bring good news to the world; they *are* good news to the world.

For Reflection

1. When you think about the preaching in your home community, is it characterized by the proclamation of the good news broadly understood? Is it shaming, judging, or

35

brow beating? Though it may be encouraging, does it have a unique gospel to offer?

2. When something is proclaimed, it is stated with a degree of confidence and directness. How might this make preaching differ from Christian education, pastoral care, or other practices such as hospitality?

3. How might your worshipping community change its preaching practice to better match the sending character of preaching?

4. Toward which of the four functions of preaching (teach, heal, save, or free) do you most naturally gravitate? From which of the four functions of preaching do you most naturally pull away? Why?

5. Run through the last year of preaching experience in your mind. Do any one of the four functions of preaching dominate? Are any missing? How would you describe the distribution of the functions in the preaching experiences you have had (both preaching your own and engaging in others' sermons)?

6. Consider using the graphic included in this chapter as a visual for eliciting feedback from your ministry team. Let them score the whole church's preaching ministry over the last few years on each function using a scale of 1 to 10. Ten equals regular, deep, and transformative engagement of that preaching function. One equals rare, if at all, engagement of any kind with that preaching function.

CHAPTER 3
What Makes a Preacher Good?

A big-steeple preacher was well received by the culture of his urban, wealthy mainline church. We can call him Peter. Peter's educational pedigree was strong, his articulation and bearing dignified, his sermons well structured and poetic. A friend invited him to preach for a suburban blue-collar church one state away and he was happy to come—until he started preaching. He could sense the disconnection with the congregation. Faces were flat, even frowning, instead of welcoming and warm. The silence after his sermon was awkward and he was glad to return home.

Peter did not realize his educational pedigree was a barrier to the people from the beginning of the introduction. Worse, he did not know to shorten that distance. Instead Peter highlighted his education in the opening illustration written in his manuscript by sharing a memory from his time in a prestigious university. His poetic prose was perceived as inauthentic and an attempt to impress. Peter's calm demeanor was not understood as dignified, but dispassionate, cool, and lacking conviction. Even his clothes communicated to the congregation that he was better than them. Peter was above them in every way and seemed to want to show it.

What was missing for this preacher? It is safe to say that something in the person of the preacher affected the preacher's decisions both in content and presentation. The internal attitudes and reactions of the preacher to the context led to many missteps. The aim of preaching was thwarted. The functions of preaching were hobbled. When a preacher lacks contextual virtues it can be difficult for preaching to accomplish its task.

What internal attitudes and habits help a preacher teach, save, heal, and free those who listen? What internal attitudes and habits block the preacher's efforts to teach, save, heal, and free others? Each of these functions can be discerned as requiring a particular internal relationship to people, scripture, theology, culture, class, gender, and so forth. Christian theology and ethics have tended to call these internal attitudes and habits virtues. For many reasons, not the least of which is the contextually rooted nature of the practice of preaching, I use the phrase *contextual virtues*.[1]

The previous chapter outlined the preacher's longing in the aim of preaching and the preacher's doing through the functions of preaching. This chapter outlines the preacher's being. A good preacher seeks to have a way of being that facilitates the enjoyment of preaching's aim and functions and the process that accomplishes them. Four contextual virtues have consistently emerged in homiletical literature across the centuries: centered humility, compassionate empathy, participatory wisdom, and courageous justice. The first three virtues are present in homiletical literature very clearly from the beginning. The history of preaching theory has often submerged the fourth virtue, courageous justice, except for in more prophetic voices. This chapter will explore the first three; the next chapter will give extended attention to the fourth.

Contextual Virtues Defined

If you have listened to very many sermons you have likely noticed one lack of contextual virtue or another. Perhaps you have attended a church only to realize the worship and preaching and culture did not embrace you, your context, or your culture's ways of life. You were not welcome there in a thousand subtle ways. Maybe you have suffered through a sermon that

---

1. For the contextually rooted practice of preaching, both skill and virtue must be deeply contextually responsive. The word *virtue* already has too much imperialistic baggage. For that reason I employ *contextual* as the primary modifier and identifier of true virtue. Pharisaical versions of virtue often miss that the refugee was hungry and needed bread (David's illegal eating of holy food) or that a young woman caught up in sexual immorality may have had no other viable option (Esther's sex slavery in Persia).

did not understand your struggles yet condemned your responses to those struggles. Have you found yourself in complete agreement with the claim of a sermon but disagreeing with its implications for the life situations of people you love? You may have also defended a preacher to a friend because he or she acted inappropriately out of ignorance for the context. If you have experienced any of these, you have recognized the need for contextual virtues.

A contextual virtue is *a core of contextually responsive habits and intentions that enables a person to enjoy an intrinsically good way of life.* When contextual virtues are absent, achievement of the internal goods of practices tends to be diminished or blocked.[2] A good kind of preaching life becomes inaccessible in spite of engagement with the external actions of preaching when contextual virtues are absent. A preacher can "make do," but a preacher will not enjoy all the preaching life can offer and the congregation will not receive all that preaching can bring. The following paragraphs give a little more detail to each part of this definition before turning to specific contextual virtues preaching theory continues to affirm.

Contextual virtues are defined as *contextually responsive* in two primary ways. First, the virtue is a contextual virtue because its core characteristics center on a particular kind of loving response to context. The virtue is contextually responsive in its essential nature. Second, the virtue is a contextual virtue because it is expressed differently in diverse contexts. Therefore, the internal reality of the contextual virtue is a definable but not always discernible phenomenon. A person can master the external appearances of the virtue while not obtaining the internal reality. Only a change of contexts (changing churches, guest preaching, new diversity in listeners, untouched topics) in which different external reactions are required would reveal the lack of virtue.

---

2. The persistent addition of the adjective *contextual* to virtues indicates my primary critique and discomfort with MacIntyre's project. This definition blends Aristotle's *hexis* (active condition of the soul) with Alasdair MacIntyre's "internal goods" and Dewey's more sophisticated naturalistic understanding of integrated habits and character. With the phrase *way of life* I intend to indicate that virtues are not *only* exercised in isolated practices but also interpenetrate all spheres of life in reinforcing and rupturing ways. See Alasdair MacIntrye, *After Virtue: A Study in Moral Theory*, 2nd ed. (Notre Dame, IN: University of Notre Dame Press, 1984), 186–89; and John Dewey, *Democracy and Education* (New York: The Free Press, 1966).

A contextual virtue offers *a responsive core of habits and intentions*. Part of the effectiveness of the practice of preaching is its across-time nature. Therefore, the most important measure of the person of the preacher is not his momentary way of being for a particular sermon. It is a preacher's motivation, intention, and habitual way of acting and being as she lives the preaching life that matters deeply. This web of internal realities and externalized habits cannot be disentangled from the rest of life. This is part of the reason for the old preaching proverb of a young preacher asking a sixty-year-old preacher, "How long did it take you to prepare that sermon?" The experienced preacher ponders and replies, "Sixty years."

This also means that a contextual virtue is regularly exercised, if it is truly virtuous. Contextual virtues are active qualities a person demonstrates, rather than static possessions a preacher can "own." Aristotle's description of virtue as an active condition of the soul, like an inward muscle, is apt. If they are not demonstrated they are to some degree lacking, weak, or atrophied. This means virtue is not something one can purchase, hold, and store away in the closet of the heart. A particular virtue is an integral part of who we are, regularly practiced and nurtured. The degree to which it is integrated across life's many contexts is the determining factor of a contextual virtue's strength.

Contextual virtues help us *enjoy an intrinsically good way of life*. The regular exercise of something such as compassionate empathy enriches our lives, not just preaching. Preparing to preach becomes a good practice ground for life just as a contextually virtuous life is a crucial source of understanding for preaching. However, if we only "turn on" the skill sets of appearing virtuous when preparing to preach we neither enjoy a good way of life nor benefit fully in our ability to preach well. If, however, compassionate empathy (or the other virtues) becomes an integral habitual way of being, all of life is able to enrich preaching in the most meaningful ways.

Finally, a contextual virtue is *necessarily attentive to and embodied in concrete contexts*. To claim a virtue, define a virtue, or give abstract examples of how virtues look is not the same as being virtuous. The embodied and culturally responsive nature of contextual virtues, not merely their definition, is necessary for their existence. A preacher is virtuous insofar as she embodies love in culturally responsive ways across diverse contexts over time. Contextual virtues are enacted differently in different contexts, but the internal intentions and habits that lead to the response remain the same.

It is a misnomer to suggest that a virtuous person acts the same in all times, all places, and all situations. This becomes clearly true in situations that force people to actively engage difference ("cross-cultural," "cross-class," "cross-gender," and so forth). An action that appears grateful in one social class will appear greedy in another. Consider the example of the North American white male who feels it is his job to eat heartily any food that is put in front of him as a sign of gratitude. In some tribes in South America the greatest sin is that of the "meat glutton." The same action in two different contexts appears grateful in one and greedy in another. The humble and empathetic person will consistently listen, learn, and lovingly change her way of acting toward others based on the context.

With contextual virtues defined in general, it is time to describe preaching's particular contextual virtues in specific. Clyde Fant claimed, "Listing character traits needed by the preacher is exactly as futile as listing the attributes of God . . . and for the same reason . . . [the listings] generally become superficial and usually wind up sounding like the Boy Scout oath, 'Brave, clean, and reverent.'"[3] This is true since to be a good preacher, one would ideally be a good person. In order to avoid the generality that plagues any attempt to be "complete" in discussions of the preacher's person, we must ask which contextual virtues are inherently necessary for preaching to be good due to its aim and functions.[4] A focused review of the most influential preaching texts of Christian history reveals four virtues that persistently emerge and also move beyond the superficiality of childhood oaths.[5] The preacher who seeks to exercise these virtues will move further toward truly good preaching than the preacher who seeks skills alone.

---

3. Clyde E. Fant, *Preaching for Today*, 1st ed. (New York: Harper & Row Publishers, 1975), 59.

4. A full review of the history of homiletical literature is impossible. The volumes written on preaching multiply by the year. I trust the reader to know that a focused review across the history of homiletics has shaped and guided this section more than the text or even the footnotes will reveal.

5. In keeping with the historical descriptive process in the last chapter, this chapter begins with Augustine as the initial and most enduring full text on Christian preaching. Augustine's conclusions are confirmed, modified, or discarded depending on insights into preaching from ensuing centuries.

Centered Humility

The history of homiletics from the time of Augustine through the modern era places a high premium on humility in the preacher. Augustine places humility as the central virtue in all of his writings. This is likely because of the central role pride and humility play in his theological anthropology and conceptions of sin.[6] His conception of humility was not abstract, however, but based on his claim that Christ is the "model, pattern and doctor of all humility" for ministry.[7]

Augustine has good reasons for beginning his preaching textbook with concerns for humility in the reader. First of all, preaching is not something that one can learn by mastering skills and overcoming personal weaknesses. There are incapacities in the preacher that only God can help one overcome. Preachers know this in their bones—we cannot do what we must. Preaching is beyond us and yet always before us, necessary and impossible. Therefore, a humble dependence on the Spirit of God is crucial to the preacher's sense of well-being in the preaching life.

The second characteristic of humility for Augustine comes in the form of teachability. The preacher must be able to learn without pride (*sine superbia*) or jealousy. Augustine is concerned that the prideful mind and heart of the overly confident preacher could both thwart the capacity to be changed by the perspective of another (including Augustine's writings) and prevent the preacher from improving either spiritually or performatively. Pride, as it is traditionally understood, often leads us to think we know better than others what is true, what is better, or what will work. Preachers who cannot receive differing opinions from others will find it very difficult to grow as preachers across their ministry lives.

The preaching life is a teachable life. Good preachers are taught not only how to preach better by inner reflection and communal feedback but also how to understand God better as one text challenges another, one neighbor's view ruptures another, and all of these things challenge our souls. It would be difficult to think of two more important internal

---

6. This emphasis is even stronger in Augustine's explorations of ordained ministerial roles.

7. Lee Francis Bacchi, *The Theology of Ordained Ministry in the Letters of Augustine of Hippo* (San Francisco: International Scholars Publications, 1998).

qualities for the long haul of a preaching life than spiritual dependence and teachability.[8] Any qualities that come to mind would eventually suffer or at least be limited by a lack of those two things. These two make up the core of humility.

Augustine's instinct to center humility in the person of Christ is also important for this discussion. A centering of the Christian virtue of humility in the person of Christ makes the use of humility for oppressive means out of bounds. Christ was the oppressed and identified with the oppressed, not the other way around. Further, the scriptural Christ's example is far from passive or codependent. The confident presence in the courageous person of Christ gives humility a nameable center. The Christ who actively unmasked the abuses of privilege and power from a position of poverty and oppression makes the golden mean of humility concretely graspable.[9] Neither in passive shame nor in overweening pride, the Christian formed in centered humility follows after Christ in proclaiming good news to the poor, freedom for the captives.

The need for humility is not mentioned in Augustine alone. The great preaching movements of the Middle Ages were the mendicant friars whose habit and habits were bent toward outward and inward humility. Luther counsels preachers to delight most if in scriptural interpretation "things develop counter to one's intentions."[10] This after all is the mark that scriptures have spoken to the preacher with a voice of their own.

The reformers in the sixteenth through seventeenth centuries emphasized humility sometimes to a fault. Calvin is famously known to quote Augustine in claiming that humility is first, second, and third in Christianity. He describes humility in his commentary on Matthew 18:4 by stating a person "is truly humble who neither claims any personal merit in the sight of God, nor proudly despises brethren, or aims at being

---

8. Preaching apprenticeships, sermon feedback forms, preaching coaching, and peer-based preaching groups all require teachability to reach their aim.

9. Consider the cleansing of the temple that occurs in all four Gospels, the liberative purpose announced in Luke 4:14-31, or Christ's many prophetic actions on behalf of women. For the latter, see Ben Witherington III, *Women in the Ministry of Jesus: A Study of Jesus' Attitudes to Women and Their Roles as Reflected in His Earthly Life* (Cambridge: Cambridge University Press, 1984).

10. Martin Luther, *Faith in Luther: Martin Luther and the Origin of Anthropocentric Religion* (Chicago: Franciscan Herald Press, 1970), 76.

thought superior to them, but reckons it enough that he is one of the members of Christ, and desires nothing more than that the Head alone should be exalted."[11]

The prideful preacher then would presume that she has something to offer on her own, without help from God or others, and seek the praise she wants to merit from others. The prideful preacher seeks to be seen as better than or superior to other followers of God. The prideful preacher desires many things more than the doxological life. After all, this preacher longs for a glory of her own.

Gardner C. Taylor, often named the dean of black preaching, argued that humility was the first and foremost virtue a preacher must develop.[12] James Earl Massey presented to his followers the same conclusion. Fred Craddock, the widely influential representative of the New Homiletic, based his transformative theory of preaching around the cultural humbling of the pastor. He counseled us that the "old thunderbolts lie rusting in the attic" and that even a "soft authoritarianism" cannot be retained if the postmodern preacher is to be heard.[13] A certain type of humility—one that extends all the way to uncertainty about the way the sermon will finally be completed in the lives of the people—is required.

Even homileticians who seem to argue against humility are actually arguing against a-contextual versions of humility that are primarily the dominant group's subconscious attempts to oppress others. Cleophus LaRue argues for a centered humility in which a preacher is confident but not arrogant. This preacher helps to raise the self-esteem of a congregation with a shame-free cultural self-identity.[14] It is not centered humility he condemns but false humility. John McClure in *Other-wise Preaching* argues for a kind of humility that sacrifices the ego of the majority-group preacher. The preacher is required to seek ongoing rupture and dislocation

11. John Calvin, *Commentary on the Harmony of the Gospels: Matthew, Mark, and Luke*, vol. 2, trans. William Pringle (Edinburgh: Edinburgh Printing Company, 1845), 333.

12. Gardner C. Taylor, *How Shall They Preach?* (Elgin, IL: Progressive Baptist Publishing House, 1977), 30–31.

13. Fred Craddock, *As One without Authority* (St. Louis: Chalice Press, 2001), 13.

14. Cleophas J. LaRue, *The Heart of Black Preaching*, (Louisville, KY: John Knox Press, 2000), 107, 121–122.

of formerly rigid ideas for the sake of others. This sense of dependence and teachability is radicalized in McClure's thought to the point of self-erasure. Though McClure would likely critique much of virtue theory, his reflections point to a more radical humility than even virtue theory typically requires.[15]

Seeking this virtue is particularly necessary for members of dominant, privileged groups (white, male, middle class and upper class, North American, Western, ruling elites of any society such as Rajanyas in India, persons from historically well-educated families, and so forth). Otherwise, as Justo González would warn, pride subtly poisons preaching by "an unconscious process through which the values, goals, and interests of those in power are read into scripture."[16] It is a tragic irony that often those communities who fear *eisegesis* the most, often practice it automatically.[17]

There may be no set of homileticians more nervous of humility than those who deeply engage Christian feminism. It would be expected for humility to be rejected, not celebrated. Rebecca Chopp, a feminist homiletician, when understood well, actually argues for a centered humility rather than a false or debased version. First and foremost, the preacher needs to lift the oppressed preacher to an awareness of her power to speak in her uniqueness.[18] Centered humility is likely reached from below for the embattled woman preacher when the preacher's view of self is lifted rather than lowered, empowered rather than weakened. Second, Chopp seeks to describe the bourgeois male condition as one who was "promised freedom in his autonomy" yet "discovers few genuine possibilities for the

---

15. John McClure, *Other-wise Preaching: A Postmodern Ethic for Homiletics* (St. Louis: Chalice Press, 2001), 4–6. McClure argues for a radical erasure of the ego in the preacher. He may presume the preacher is privileged and likely male. McClure's work would not in any intentional way suggest erasure of minority voice.

16. Justo L. González and Catherine Gunsalus González, *Liberation Preaching: The Pulpit and the Oppressed* (Nashville: Abingdon Press, 1980). González and González also warn preachers to recognize their mixed relationship to power privileged. The white female is in a position of oppression due to sexism but a position of privilege or power due to white privilege.

17. *Eisegesis* means putting meaning "into" (Greek root *eis*) the text versus pulling meaning out of (Greek root *ex*) the text, which is *exegesis*.

18. Chopp states, "Despite the influx of women into leadership roles in the church and teaching roles in the academy, I am not sure women's 'otherness' is either heard or spoken" (*Power to Speak: Feminism, Language, God* [New York: Crossroad, 1989]), 7.

community, relationships, and love he so desires."[19] For one, centered humility will require a new "willingness to let one's mind be changed."[20] For another, centered humility requires "the willingness to make one's own opinion, argument, and knowledge available."[21]

This brief overview of diverse homileticians across the history of homiletics is in no way comprehensive. The diversity of time period, geographical context, ethnic background, and theological tradition serves to show that centered humility is a perpetually core virtue in the minds of expert preachers and teachers of preaching. It is first if not foremost in the pantheon of preaching virtues.

What characterizes a preacher with centered humility? This limited survey of homiletics also helps populate the content of what is meant by centered humility. The preacher who has a habit of centered humility approaches interpretation in certain ways. The preacher recognizes her own voice and insights, neither discarding them as irrelevant nor imagining them to be self-sufficient. The preacher engages the text as a voice that is expected to surprise, undo, and overturn. The overarching attitude of the humble preacher is teachability but not without questioning. The preacher does not lose the self simply because sacred scripture is being read. The preacher who regularly goes to scripture with a teachable mind, who has a habit of spiritual dependence, who seeks out diverse and unsettling perspectives, who maintains a sense of self but allows that self to be undone and redone is experiencing centered humility. In delivery the humble preacher does not condescend, preaching as though "people" struggle but the pastor knows the better way. Nor does the humble preacher cower and self-deprecate as though he does not have anything to say. Instead, as a fellow pilgrim leading for a day, the preacher guides the listener on a journey of mutual discovery and experience of the presence of God.

---

19. Ibid., 68.
20. Ibid., 97.
21. Ibid.

Compassionate Empathy

If humility leans toward others, empathy is the internal embrace of others. Humility seeks the perspectives of others out of a willing acknowledgment of lack or need. Empathy embraces the experiences of others out of compassion, care, and concern. It is one thing to listen, attend to, and know that you need the perspective of others. It is another to feel with, suffer for, and seek active ways to care for suffering others. Though leadership has emerged as the preeminent concern of many pastors in Western contexts in recent decades, the history of pastoral ministry places two other concerns as central: preaching and pastoral care. It is in compassionate empathy that the connection between the two becomes clear.

Empathy is composed of two major components.[22] The first is cognitive, and the second affective or emotive. *Cognitive* empathy is a matter of being attuned to another's perspective or their horizon of perspective in its emotional reality. *Affective* empathy exhibits an appropriate emotional response. This divides what may not be able to be so neatly divided. Cognitive attunement without proper affective response is the definition of sociopathology. For emotionally healthy humans, the cognitive and affective dimensions are not so easily divided. This is why the modifier "compassionate" is so important for preaching's view of empathy. It is a chilling thought to imagine preachers understanding the emotional worlds of others in arms-length, emotion-free analysis for the sake of their own benefit. All of the above helps to define compassionate empathy as *the habitual tendency (whether spontaneous or intentional) to embrace multiple others' experiences with an appropriate emotional response motivated by concern for the other's well-being.*

Compassionate empathy is central to theories of preaching from the earliest days in similar ways to centered humility. The strengthening of the "bonds of love" between preacher and God, preacher and listener,

---

22. See Heinz Kohut, "On Empathy" and "Introspection, Empathy and the Semicircle of Mental Health" in *The Search for the Self: Selected Writings of Heinz Kohut: 1978–1981*, ed. P. H. Orstein (Madison, WI: International Universities Press, 1981), 525–35 and 537–67 respectively. Or see Martha Craven Nussbaum, *Upheavels of Thought: The Intelligence of Emotions* (Cambridge: Cambridge University Press, 2001), 304–35 for a rhetorical perspective. For a critique of gendered views of empathy, see Cordelia Fine, *Delusions of Gender: How Our Minds, Society, and Neurosexism Create Difference* (New York: W. W. Norton & Company, 2011).

and listener and God is one of the primary results of preaching for Augustine.[23] Whereas humility was directed both vertically and horizontally, for Augustine, compassion primarily emphasizes horizontal relationships with other human beings.

One of the most important themes in Augustine's work related to empathy is the "counsel of compassion" (*consilium misericordiae*). In his seven-stage exposition of the ascent toward wisdom, step four is the counsel of compassion *consilium misericordiae*.[24] Analyzing Augustine's discussions of compassionate empathy (*misericordia*) reveals two characteristics. The first characteristic is the attendance to and discernment of real human needs (cognitive). Second is the deeply felt desire to meet needs or direct the neighbor toward the appropriate fulfillment of needs (affective). This means that, for Augustine, compassionate empathy is not merely a skill one masters but a way of being that requires the whole person (cognition, affect, and volition). Further, it is central to the progress toward the kind of wisdom preaching requires. Compassionate empathy guides the preacher and informs the preacher.

Augustine's view of compassionate empathy was not unique in the early church. Gregory of Nyssa's sermons, letters, and writings emphasized the need for compassion in preaching. Maximus, the confessor in later centuries, articulated both elements of compassionate empathy, effective and cognitive, as crucial to both Christian action and Christian preaching. Gregory the Great in his book of pastoral rule gives such emphasis to compassion and empathy that he also offers concern for something that we would now call compassion fatigue.[25]

---

23. This is Hughes Oliphant Old's interpretation of Augustine's doxological aim of preaching. Old also sees Augustine's doxological aim for preaching as both vertical and horizontal in *Reading and Preaching of the Scriptures*, 2:388.

24. Augustine, *On Christian Teaching*, trans. R. P. H. Green (New York: Oxford University Press, 1997), 34 (1.10.10). Green translates *consilium misericordia* as "the resolve of compassion," emphasizing the volitional aspect of the characteristic that Augustine describes earlier as the desire to meet real needs of the neighbor. This is an understandable and possible translation, though it is the least likely meaning of the Latin term. It would better be translated as the "counsel of compassion." This usage is justified in Latin and better matches the use of Isaiah 11:2 by Augustine in which counsel/advice is in view (*etzah*). This is further strengthened contextually with *sapientia* or wisdom as the aim of *consilium*.

25. For a more thorough investigation of the emphasis on compassion in the early church, read Susan Wessel, *Passion and Compassion in Early Christianity* (Cambridge: Cambridge University Press, 2016). This fascinating and thorough work confirms that compassion was much more central to the lived life of the early church than it is to the Western contemporary church.

In more recent homiletical thought subtle echoes and explicit descriptions of compassionate empathy abound. If the first three chapters of *As One without Authority* can be read productively as a theological and methodological call for humility, the fourth chapter, "Inductive Preaching and the Imagination," is an explicit summons for compassionate empathy. Repeatedly throughout the chapter when Craddock mentions imagination in preaching his fuller label is "empathetic imagination."[26] In Craddock's theory, empathetic imagination is logically essential to the practice of preaching he envisions.

It should be evident how indispensable to preaching, and most especially inductive preaching, is the pastoral involvement in the life of the congregation. When the pastor writes a sermon, an empathetic imagination sees again those concrete experiences with people that called on all her resources, drove her to the Bible and back again, and even now hang as vivid pictures in her mind.[27]

Pastoral care is not sermon preparation any more than all of life prepares the person of the preacher for preaching. The empathetic preacher does not make listeners feel used by retelling the story from last night's dinner table or hospital bed. All of this is Craddock's modern way of communicating the need for the accumulation of a "counsel of compassion" in the life of the preacher.

Given the postmodern critique of empathy, one expects more hesitancy in later homileticians when speaking of compassion. While hesitation is there, in each project it eventually becomes clear that the thinker is critiquing the *misuse* of empathy not its proper use. In *The Power to Speak*, Rebecca Chopp functionally celebrates a non-essentialized concept of the state of empathy.[28] She celebrates "the wide-awakefulness of empathy as

---

26. Craddock, *As One without Authority*, 67, 70, and 73.

27. Ibid., 67. Without careful attendance to life, one is not fully prepared to preach. At the same time, the empathetic impressions from life are not to be immediately dropped into a barrel of sermon illustrations. The concrete images left from empathetic memory hang "as vivid pictures" in the mind of the preacher but are only rarely used as sermonic material. They are formative in a more holistic way, affecting preaching indirectly and cumulatively rather than directly and with immediacy.

28. For a broader historical exploration of this Third Wave Feminist critique of Second Wave Feminist essentialism, as well as a critique of the categories Third Wave and Second Wave themselves, see Nancy Hewitt, *No Permanent Waves: Recasting Histories of U.S. Feminism* (New Brunswick: Rutgers University Press, 2010), 109–13.

really understanding how others feel and live their lives, not simply how we would feel if we lived their lives."[29] John McClure states that his view of other-wise preaching has to be "motivated and sustained by an *ethical* concern to reorient preaching toward the 'other,' to situate preaching as a radical act of compassionate responsibility."[30]

Alyce McKenzie's *Hear and Be Wise* sketches the broad contours of centered humility and compassionate empathy as the precursors to wisdom.[31] McKenzie outlines them as pillars that help to hold up the roof of wisdom. For McKenzie the one who preaches with "bended knee" has one of the pillars of wisdom. This image of the bended knee is explicated in ways parallel to the concept of centered humility. McKenzie's image of the preacher who preaches with a "listening heart" explicitly mentions compassionate and empathetic listening as another pillar of wisdom. This explanation of preaching's contextual virtues is not concerned with the labels for the virtues[32] but the continual expression of the same reality under different names and verbiage. McKenzie's elevation of the preacher as sage, or wise one, foreshadows the next contextual virtue while confirming the first two as central to preaching. This is a recurring theme in preaching literature: humility leads to empathy, and empathy leads to wisdom.

Taylor sees empathy's relation to the practice of preaching in a parallel way to centered humility. These virtues are both prerequisites and consequences of the practice of preaching. Even in his lecture on "building a sermon," Taylor's most skill-oriented lecture, he finds it "necessary to comment on our grasp of the Bible *by way of the human condition*."[33] The preacher is charged to come to "know the doubts and hopes, the longings and fears, the strengths and weaknesses of the human heart."[34] In the same section

---

29. Rebecca S. Chopp, "Remarks Delivered by Colgate University President Institute on College Student Values Conference Tallahassee" (Colgate University President Institute on College Student Values Conference, Tallahassee, FL, February 3, 2006).

30. McClure, *Other-wise Preaching*, 7.

31. Alyce M. McKenzie, *Hear and Be Wise: Becoming a Preacher and Teacher of Wisdom* (Nashville: Abingdon Press, 2010).

32. For example, is it wisdom *as* bended knee or centered humility as a precursor to wisdom?

33. Taylor, *How Shall They Preach?* 65. Emphasis added.

34. Ibid.

Taylor goes on to indicate that this empathetic way of knowing emerges first through honest and self-accepting self-awareness. The honest embrace of self is the first step toward not only centered humility but also compassionate empathy. In Taylor's reading of a sampling of "great preachers" they were "in touch with the deepest sources of themselves" and so were better able to touch the deepest portions of others.[35] Only this kind of centered humility and compassionate empathy is able to produce "deep and searching preaching" that gets at the "deepest and most vulnerable places of other peoples' hurt hearts."[36] This preaching does not simply put the finger where it already hurts, pressing on the bruise. Rather the preacher "speaks to them with divine pity which weeps . . . at the same time in which it challenges."[37] There is no question that compassionate empathy is in view.

Cleophus LaRue again offers a perspective on empathy in the historically black church in North America. "To preach black," LaRue asserts, "is to preach out of an awareness of the issues and concerns of life with which blacks struggle and contend daily. The black sermon at its best arises out of the totality of the people's existence—their pain and joy, trouble and ecstasy."[38] This diverse awareness of African American experiences forms LaRue's version of Augustine's counsel of compassion or Craddock's empathetic imagination. To lack this empathetic awareness, then, is not only to fail to "connect" with a congregation. More important, this lack of empathy is to fail to understand scripture from an African American perspective. Without empathy the content changes, not only the delivery. An empathy-shaped lens forms the way the pastor interprets scripture.

If space and time allowed, a more thorough overview of compassionate empathy in homiletics would be instructive and helpful for the preacher and the teacher of preaching.[39] It is beyond the scope of this book. Once

---

35. Ibid., 65–67.

36. Ibid., 72.

37. Ibid., 83.

38. Cleophus LaRue, *The Heart of Black Preaching*, 6.

39. One example was released after this manuscript was submitted and edited, not allowing for any extended treatment. See my colleague Lenny Luchetti's, *Preaching with Empathy*, Artistry of Preaching Series, ed. Paul Scott Wilson (Nashville: Abingdon Press, 2018). May the homiletical literature on each of these virtues continue to abound.

we are convinced of the need for empathy, we need to discern what it looks like particularly in the preaching life.

A brief sketch of the preacher who exercises compassionate empathy may help.[40] A preacher who has compassionate empathy is one who is regularly engaged in the joys and sorrows of others, listens with caring interest, seeks to discern others' real experience, and does not project her own emotions onto others. He builds from a strong self-awareness toward others-awareness with a desire to meet real physical, social, and spiritual needs. The preacher who has compassionate empathy might hear someone say his preaching feels like "hearing someone read my journal back to me," that her preaching "touched me deeply at the place where I hurt the most," that his words were healing not merely instructive, or that the prescriptions she gives for human conditions are "deep medicine for the soul."

Participatory Wisdom

When you live through even one northern winter in a drafty home, a longing for fire is very understandable. After receiving a rather expensive quote on a fireplace for our home, I decided it could not be all *that* difficult to build a fireplace. With a brief search, I found an online guide to building a fireplace in a weekend—just eleven steps. The steps were easy to understand, but I am no fool. I announced it would take me three or four weeks to build the fireplace, not the weekend the article so casually suggested. *Four months* later the paint was not yet dry and the plumber connected the gas line to the fireplace. I understood how to build a fireplace when I thought one month was more than enough. However, now I have something more than understanding, I have hard-earned wisdom.

There is a knowing that comes only from the inside of a thing. This is the difference between what the ancients called *scientia* from which we get the word *science*, and *sapientia* from which we get the phrase *sapient being*.

---

40. For a pastorally minded work that explores how to preach from the basis of ongoing compassionate empathy, see LeRoy Aden and Robert G. Hughes, *Preaching God's Compassion: Comforting Those Who Suffer* (Minneapolis: Fortress Press, 2001). Also see Donald Capps's great work, *Pastoral Counseling and Preaching: A Quest for an Integrated Ministry* (Philadelphia; Westminster, 1980).

To know from the outside is *scientia*, a studied observation. To know from experience within is wisdom. There are preachers who study the Scriptures and then preach them as an eleven-step process for building the fireplace they themselves have never quite come around to building. They do not have *participatory wisdom*.[41]

For preaching, participatory wisdom can be defined as *experiential understanding resulting from the holistic engagement with the subject in diverse contexts of life*. This experiential understanding comes first through vicarious experience and reflection (humility and empathy) and then through direct engagement and personal reflection (participatory wisdom). Not only is the preacher offering wisdom for life she herself discovered originally. But also she is giving witness to the life others handed to her through the writings of scripture, the teaching of the church in its many forms, Christian community as it engages the world, the broader cultures she engages, and more. No human lives long enough to gain as much wisdom alone as she could gain more quickly through humility and empathy.

Homiletics consistently affirms participatory wisdom, described in various ways, throughout the history of its development. Beginning again with Augustine's work, *On Christian Teaching*, we find that the first homiletics textbook strongly emphasizes participatory wisdom for the preacher. Augustine's view of Christian wisdom is measured not merely by knowing about the canon of scripture. He desires "real understanding and careful investigation of [the Scriptures'] meaning" to which he attaches the importance of attendance to the Scriptures not only intellectually, but also with the lived life of the preacher.[42] Preachers who are not yet seeking to embody in some living way the gospel they encounter through the text have not yet fully grasped or gained wisdom from that gospel. They may know its structure intellectually, but they do not understand its import existentially. The word of God speaks from deep to deep. The unengaged preacher is only able to preach from exterior to exterior, surface

---

41.   The latter half of this book will offer a rhythm of the preaching life that allows for wisdom to take better hold before preaching gains voice. A monthly pattern for preaching is far superior to a weekly one when wisdom (not just a creative sermon) is the desire.

42.   Augustine, *On Christian Teaching*, 104 (4.5.7).

to surface. The engaged preacher resonates from interior to interior, while still expressing and addressing the exterior of text, meaning, experience, and life.

In chapter 1, homiletical Donatism and Docetism were outlined as two poles of wrong thinking for preaching. Augustine avoids both of these practical theological missteps by his unique relationship between wisdom and eloquence. It is the *pursuit of* wisdom and the *use of* eloquence that are precisely the responsibility of the preacher in Augustine's mind. It is inspired transformation of will and action for the preacher (during the pursuit) and for the listener (during the sermon) that is the domain of God. This maintains responsibility on the part of the human but ascribes ownership of positive results to God.

Here again Augustine emphasizes the interiority of the speaker. Rather than observation of external rules, or packaging of concepts with ornamental words, Augustine suggests a movement with energized resonance from the interiority of the preacher through the spoken words to the interiority of the listener. This passionate nature—an ability to be appropriately moved and to appropriately move another—is central to Augustine's homiletical rhetoric.[43] This is also true for *doctrina*, a term that often carries the subtle meaning of "habit formed by teaching."[44] This means that Augustine believes eloquence emerges most naturally when the content of the sermon has changed the attitudes and habits of the preacher.

In classical rhetorical categories, Augustine has emphasized participatory wisdom over knowledge (*logos*), the lived life over the projected image, as well as compassion instead of command and control (*ethos*), and now

---

43. Even the three rhetorical styles taken from Cicero are outlined not primarily in terms of their ornamental elements but by their level of passionate engagement. As John Schaeffer has argued, in both Augustine's *De doctrina Christiana* and Augustine's preaching practice, "wisdom and eloquence are synthesized in an extemporaneous oral performance that emerges from the preacher's interiority, that is, from an authentic self, formed by doctrine." (John D. Schaeffer, "The Dialectic of Orality and Literacy: The Case of Book 4 of Augustine's *De doctrina Christiana*," Publications of the Modern Language Association 111, no. 5 (1996): 1137.

44. *De doctrina Christiana* is the title of Augustine's preaching textbook. *Doctrina* is often translated "doctrine" or "teaching." See E. A. Andrews, *A Copious and Critical Latin-English Lexicon: Founded on the Larger Latin-German Lexicon of Dr. William Freund; with Additions and Corrections from the Lexicons of Gesner, Facciolati, Scheller, Georges, Etc.* (New York: Harper & Brothers, 1851), 496 (doctrina, II.B).

authentic psycho-emotional energy over stylistic embellishment (*pathos*). In the first two, wisdom and the lived life (*logos, ethos*), he has greatly welded wisdom to active engagement with the faith.[45] In the final two, the lived life and authentic emotion (*ethos, pathos*), he has dethroned the importance of *eloquentia*, putting participatory wisdom in its place.

Throughout the history of Christian reflection on preaching the participation of the preacher in the life proclaimed is paramount. Gregory states that anyone who speaks the word of God should first "consider his own manner of life." Referencing Gregory, Humbert of Romans adds, "goodness of life is necessary for every preacher."[46] The emphasis on the participation of the preacher in the Christian life proclaimed is so strong in the great awakenings as to nearly go without comment.[47] Yet this emphasis is not secluded to the histories of preaching long gone. Recent homileticians consistently emphasize it as well.

The overlapping nature of the aim, functions, and contextual virtues for preaching is striking in a few of Fred Craddock's allusions to participation and the wisdom it brings. He asks the rhetorical question, "Does one preach on a text, or get into it, listen to it, and share what is heard?"[48] Craddock assumes preachers will be "thrilled, frightened, moved, paralyzed, honored, humbled, and inescapably addressed" by their ongoing interaction with the Scriptures and God's call.[49] Most instructively he sees the busy pastor's involvement as an asset, not a liability, to wisdom in proclaiming scripture since doing is also a way of knowing. "To the extent that the minister gives herself to that same mission in the world, she will harvest a clarity of understanding texts that arise[s] out of that mission."[50] Participatory involvement with the mission scripture records gives the

---

45. This should not be mistaken to mean moral perfection or flawlessness. Rather the words *active engagement* denote involvement and intention that may very well be deeply flawed.

46. As translated in Simon Tugwell, *Early Dominicans: Selected Writings* (New York: Paulist Press, 1982), 215.

47. Certainly at times this emphasis became Donatistic and overly pietistic in tone.

48. Craddock, *As One without Authority*, 111.

49. Ibid.

50. Ibid., 112. The singular form of *arise* appears to be what Craddock intends. Without this typographical adjustment the sentence struggles to be clear.

minister clarity of insight, depth of understanding, or, in short, something to say. The preacher does not merely send a doxological community into the world but sends herself as one member of that doxological community into the world. Her engagement with the mission as it is revealed in the text for the day is a key portion of her possibility for wisdom in the day.

This is not an idiosyncratic conviction of Craddock's, opposed to the major currents of homiletical theory in the 1970s. Rather, this view of wisdom arises naturally out of the primary commitments of the New Homiletic. As James Kay writes, "the greatest contribution of the New Hermeneutic school to homiletics was in its insistence that preaching is not simply a matter of signifying the Word of God, but rather it is *participation* in the event of the Word of God."[51] This hermeneutic rooted in Heideggerian philosophy seeks to avoid all "idle talk" that emerges from a misconception that views words as containers of content to be unpacked.[52] Scriptures are sites of previous experiences with the living Word. These Word-events need to be released anew for the preacher and then released anew for the hearer. This requires a greater level of participation in preaching preparation and the preaching moment by the actual person of the preacher not necessarily required by more propositional views of preaching.[53]

In recent homiletics several works stand out as calls toward the participatory wisdom that has been historically central to advice for preachers. First, Richard Thulin, in *The "I" of the Sermon: Autobiography in the Sermon*, offers a particular test case that demonstrates all three of the aforementioned contextual virtues in one recurring concern for preaching: the preacher's personal reference. He offers three abuses of the personal pronoun that demonstrate why not just any use of first-person narrative will be helpful for preaching: (1) *Narcissistic proclamation of the self* as the model instead of Christ (a lack of centered humility). (2) *Privatistic*

---

51. James F. Kay, *Preaching and Theology* (St. Louis: Chalice Press, 2007), 100–101. Emphasis added.

52. Gerhard Ebeling, *The Nature of Faith*, trans. Ronald Gregor Smith (Philadelphia: Fortress Press, 1961), 187. Here Ebeling states, "We do not get at the nature of words by asking what they contain, but by asking what they effect, what they set going, what future they disclose."

53. Propositional preaching begins to a great degree with John Broadus's *Treatise on the Preparation and Delivery of Sermons*, 1st ed. (Philadelphia: Smith, English and Co., 1870).

personal reference with which the listener does not identify or resonate (a lack of true compassionate empathy). (3) *Disconnected self-reference* in which the sermon content itself does not relate to the revelation of the preacher's life. This lack of participatory wisdom fails to demonstrate to the listener that the preacher has sought to practice and understand from the inside out what is proclaimed. Thulin states, "What catches the ear and urges response is the voice of a living witness . . . that speaks the truth about one's life . . . a voice of conviction supported by a life story" whether or not that story is shared in the pulpit.[54] Thulin goes so far as to claim that the preacher cannot truly understand the content of a sermon unless it is anchored in lived experience. Without participation there is no true wisdom.

John McClure's *Other-wise Preaching* argues for a radical exiting of the sources of authority and wisdom (scripture, reason, tradition, and experience). Though the project seeks to be a radical postmodern view of preaching, the echoes of wisdom are not silenced nor are they meant to be. His wedding of compassionate empathy and participatory wisdom, though unique in its expression and philosophy, supports rather than rejects the notions this chapter presents. Without face-to-face interactions with others funded by humility and empathetic embrace of the other, the ruptures McClure envisions cannot happen. Without those rupturing moments, new wisdom cannot emerge. It is in the new discovery of wisdom through diverse others that preaching becomes truly *Other-wise*.

As with the first two virtues, a sketch of the preacher and her preaching life of participatory wisdom will help draw these insights together. The preacher who intentionally nurtures the virtue of participatory wisdom is not a disengaged scholar of the text. A preacher with participatory wisdom is one who wrestles with the Scriptures until the text wounds and blesses her anew, who seeks a personal word before seeking a corporate word, who ruptures her personal views through experience of the lives of others, who has participated not only in the ideas expressed in the passages but also in the reality those ideas point to in the reign of God. This preacher is a

---

54. Richard L. Thulin, *The "I" of the Sermon: Autobiography in the Sermon* (Minneapolis: Fortress Press, 1989).

preacher who participates in the life of God in the community of God in new and fresh ways, repenting anew, rejoicing anew, and bearing witness to all of this with the prudence to know what to share and what to leave by the side.

The preaching life is not meant to be one filled with the anxiety of a coming sermon, the drudgery of coming up with "something to say," or the pressure of performing a script of a character we do not know intimately. Instead, preachers can depend on God, scripture, and others to provide insights and perspectives that give the preacher something new to *live* not just something to *say*. Preachers engage in diverse communal life out of authentic compassionate concern for others, listening and learning along the way. All of this prepares the preacher to have more than an exegetical understanding of a "text." The preacher who practices the preaching life comes with an experiential understanding of wrestling with God, wrestling with scriptures, being ruptured by others, having a compassionate concern for others, and discerning an internal witness that presents itself as the word of the Lord—at the very least, a word the preacher believes would serve others well. In many ways, a preacher with these contextual virtues could stand and preach with a moment's notice a more significant sermon than the polished sermon from the professional minister who has plentiful skills but little virtue.

One of the most difficult things about helping preachers learn to preach is the necessarily interior nature of the process of preaching. Even though preachers talk with others, study metaphorically with scholars, and may even have a preaching team, much of what makes sermons sing happens within the preacher. Preaching coaches and preaching professors will often address vocal variety, authenticity of facial expression, congruence of gestures, precision of language, the gaining of interest in the introduction, or the images used throughout the sermon. Any and all of these things are important to preaching well. Still, every preaching professor or coach knows there are some things that seem unteachable—at least not in the space of a class or a coaching relationship. Those things are contextual virtues. When a person has developed them, they cover over many performative sins.

For any preacher who wants to preach well over a lifetime, acquiring contextual virtues is much more important than mastering preaching skills. If you want to grow as a preacher, you have to grow as a whole person. Seeking spiritual direction, counseling, mentoring, admitting our doubts, confessing our sins, becoming a good friend, maintaining cross-cultural relationships, listening well, practicing empathy, and engaging the life of faith (see chapter 5)—all of these things matter so very deeply for preaching. Each of these helps to form the contextual virtues the functions of preaching require. With these virtues, the slightly skillful will preach with great effect. Without these virtues, the skillful preacher will find a career, even build a ministry, but will not fully enjoy the rule of God.

For Reflection

1. Make a three-column list in which you place preachers who model each virtue. For which of these contextual virtues do you have model preachers who are from diverse ethnicities, traditions, geographical location? For which of these virtues do you have a lack of preaching models?

2. Who might be a preaching model for the virtue you long to engage most deeply? Who might others say are the models for each virtue? What practical steps can you take to learn from that diverse set of preachers?

3. Which of the three virtues mentioned above does your preaching display the least—centered humility, compassionate empathy, or participatory wisdom? If you are brave enough, have a gracious person who hears you preach tell you which comes across as your strongest and which is your weakest.

4. Few would claim contextual virtues are not helpful for preaching. After all, we notice them most when they are not there. Yet most do not mention them when thinking of what is most important for preaching practice. How would you articulate the way in which a greater awareness of the contextual virtues of preaching might aid your preaching practice?

5. Review the modifying adjective for each virtue (centered, compassionate, and participatory). Take some time to discuss with another preacher, or to journal on your own, how these modifiers can change your own pursuit of these virtues.

Courageous Justice: The Prophetic Word

I slipped my fingers into the bullet holes in the clapboard walls of the 150-year-old chapel. The building was preserved on the grounds where our youth camp was held so that we would not forget who we were. My senior pastor told the story of the early Wesleyan Methodists who went out two-by-two preaching abolition. Angry townspeople would fire through the walls into the church service. Worshipers ducked underneath the hand-hewn pews; the preacher dropped low behind the pulpit until the horsemen ran out of ammunition. Then the founders of the denomination stood back up and preached against the sins of slavery again. When I recall stories such as these, I have to ask myself whether I am just a preacher or a just preacher.

If the functions and virtues of preaching in the last few chapters were held up against the ongoing practice of preaching (its best theorists and preachers), a particular function of preaching and attendant virtue would clearly be missing. In terms of function one key biblical concept that endures throughout homiletical history remains: preaching frees captives. Jesus claims to have come "to preach good news to the poor, to proclaim release to the prisoners" (Luke 4:16). Good news to the poor and freedom for captives is a primary characteristic of preaching through the ages. Therefore, good preaching is didactic, therapeutic, soteriological, *and* liberative. It teaches, heals, saves, and frees those who have ears to hear and the will to follow.

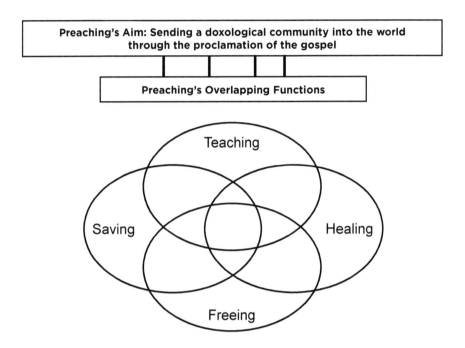

Though preachers have preached sermons that relate to freedom and justice all through Christian history, the preaching theories of homileticians have not always emphasized issues such as slavery, wrongful imprisonment, oppression, poverty, racism, sexism, violent nationalism, or the like. In other words, there has often been a gap in between the theory of preaching and the best examples of the practice of preaching.[1]

This chapter listens to the prophetic word that the historic practice of preaching can offer to homiletics. It is the same word some current homileticians are now offering back to unjust practices of preaching. It is a prophetic word that has already been heard by many preachers and teachers of preaching in the postmodern era, but not by all. The danger would be to conceive of this prophetic word only in postmodern terms. That would

---

1. This does not mean that there have not been significant gaps in practice. For example, Gregory of Nyssa decries slavery as an institution vehemently. Yet he is one of the only church fathers to do so. If he preached against it, presumably others did as well whose sermons do not survive. Yet the quietness of the church (even if not silence) on the issue of slavery is impossible to ignore. Though slavery was unaddressed, poverty and the dangers of private property were a continual theme of the preaching in the early church.

make the prophetic word a product of a particular time, philosophy, or political theory rather than what it is, an enduring characteristic of good preaching. The accompanying danger would be to assume what the terms *freedom, liberation,* or *justice* mean in the majority of Christian texts is what they mean in every Christian community or tradition. Many of the most marginalized have not been included until very recently in the texts the church has treasured and reproduced.

There are societal evils that are woven into the structure of the way a community orders life. Without some order, chaos ensues. With any form of human order, injustice is interwoven. Therefore, prophets may not be employed, but they are never without a job. These cultural forms of life trap both the powerful and the powerless in a mutually reinforcing system that is difficult to undo. Many times to speak against the evils in society is to speak against society itself in the mind of the listener. The countercultural nature of liberating preaching is therefore integral to the function. People of faith have always made it clear they are citizens of another city whose hope is not of this world and who follow authority that does not sit on human thrones. Narrowly "patriotic preachers" are contrasted with prophetic preachers in that patriotic preachers only sing the praises of the nation in which they live. Prophetic preachers sing the praises of what is good (in their nation or elsewhere) but also declare the evils of society (in their nation or elsewhere). By naming captivity, publicly calling it unjust, and demanding release of those who are held captive, preachers put "the Word before the powers"[2] and therefore stand *against* the established order. Desert prophets. Mendicants. Abolitionists. Suffragists. Civil rights prophets. These are the icons of the liberating function of preaching.

There is a long and growing tradition of naming liberating preaching as prophetic preaching. Marvin McMickle's question, "Where have all the prophets gone?" is primarily a lament of the loss of and a call to reclaim preaching for justice, for freedom.[3] Kenyatta Gilbert also calls for preaching

---

2. Charles L. Campbell, *The Word before the Powers: An Ethic of Preaching,* 1st ed. (Louisville, KY: Westminster John Knox Press, 2002).

3. Marvin McMickle, *Where Have All the Prophets Gone? Reclaiming Prophetic Preaching in America* (Cleveland, OH: Pilgrim Press, 2006).

justice in his "tri-vocal" vision of African American preachers speaking in pastoral, sagely, and prophetic voices.[4] Walter Brueggemann emphasizes the "prophetic imagination" as a resistance to the status quo and an ability to see what is not there within the preaching moment.[5] These are only a few examples of the reimaging of the preacher in the role of prophet. To think of the preacher *as* prophet is helpful since the preacher is not *only* prophet. To think of the preacher *as* prophet is dangerous in that many preachers will claim it is not their "style," not their "gift." Preachers are not called to do only that which we do best. If we preach, we are called to do what preaching does best.

Even a cursory reading of the Gospels with these thoughts in mind reveals Jesus of Nazareth as a prophetic voice. He speaks on behalf of the poor, the outcast, the racially oppressed, the religiously overburdened, the morally judged, the imprisoned, the widowed, and the invisible. No one minded Jesus reading from the prophet Isaiah. It was not until he suggested God chose individual Gentiles over all the Jews of a particular day that he was hated. The crowd is not seen upset at Jesus riding in on a donkey, that is until he cut short profit-making at the expense of the foreigner. Jesus was not condemned for eating with powerful religious leaders, but for allowing a woman to wash his feet. Jesus was not judged for failing to help prepare a meal, but for allowing a woman to act like a disciple rather than a servant. Jesus courageously risked and ultimately gave his life for the freedom of the captives and good news to the poor.

In this brief summary of Christ's liberative actions and words we see that the biblical Christ is not bound to a narrow understanding of liberation. The freeing function of preaching is also not bound to Marxist social critique or politicized versions of liberation or justice. This would be too small of a view. Christ works in his proclaimed and lived word to free people from religious prejudice (a time is coming when people

---

4. Kenyatta R. Gilbert, *The Journey and Promise of African American Preaching* (Minneapolis: Fortress Press, 2011). See also Gilbert, *Pursued Justice: Black Preaching from the Great Migration to Civil Rights* (Waco, TX: Baylor University Press, 2016). The careful reader will note the parallels with this work in the images for preaching: priestly (saving), pastoral (healing), and prophetic (freeing). The teacher has been subsumed in this tri-vocal model, but the function remains.

5. Walter Brueggemann, *The Practice of Prophetic Imagination: Preaching an Emancipating Word* (Minneapolis: Fortress Press, 2012).

will worship in spirit and in truth), moralistic legalism (is it better to do good or to do evil on the Sabbath?), economic injustice (you have made it a den of thieves), and distributive injustice (sell all you have and give it to the poor). The sources of political liberation in the biblical Christ are more subtle: the turned cheek, the tunic and the robe, the extra mile, and the refusal either to reject political authority or to bend to its claims to authority (show me a coin...my kingdom is not of this world).

Though the content-oriented themes of justice are present in every period of Christian preaching, theories of preaching do not always promote or even present them. Even though recent scholarship has gathered and examined more of Augustine's thoughts and writings on the issues of freedom and justice, it remains true that his thoughts are dissatisfying to theologians today.[6] In terms of slavery, women in society, and human rights, the vast majority of theologians and moral philosophers would find the formerly wealthy and very powerful bishop's thoughts insufficient.[7] His preaching textbook leaves concerns of economic, distributive, and retributive justice completely untouched. When Augustine focuses on what type of person a preacher ought to be (*esse debeat*), as he states his work is intended to do, liberation for captives through preaching justice is not in view.

Chrysostom's thoughts on captivity were also dual and conflicted. Though he preached often on the injustices of income disparity and inequitable wealth distribution, Chrysostom did not see clearly the great evil of society—the enslavement of brothers and sisters for the sake of economic gain. Maximus the confessor and Gregory the Great demonstrate concern for justice to individual poor and to communities that are impoverished. They do not, however, see preaching as a powerful agent of transformation for societies' injustices.

---

6. See Pauline Allen, Bronwen Neil, and Wendy Mayer, *Preaching Poverty in Late Antiquity: Perceptions and Realities* (Leipzig, Germany: Evangelische Verlagsanstalt, 2009), 143. Here the absence of the poor precisely where we expect Augustine to include them is important.

7. Teresa Delgado, John Doody, and Kim Paffenroth, *Augustine and Social Justice* (London: Lexington Books, 2015). For example, see Aaron D. Conley's essay, "Augustine and Slavery: Freedom for the Free," 131–44 in this volume in which it becomes clear that Augustine's social location as a privileged son of a slave-owning family blinds his view of the injustice to some, even while he fights the violent enslavement of formerly free persons.

Aquinas speaks eloquently on injustice in the Middle Ages in the great work he intended as a preparation manual for traveling preachers. On the virtue of justice the following passage is instructive:

> I answer that, a human virtue is one "which renders a human act and man himself good" [Ethic. ii, 6], and this can be applied to justice. For a man's [*sic*] act is made good through attaining the rule of reason, which is the rule whereby human acts are regulated. Hence, since justice regulates human operations, it is evident that it renders man's operations good, and, as Tully declares (De Officiis i, 7), good men are so called chiefly from their justice, wherefore, as he says again (De Officiis i, 7) "the luster of virtue *appears above all in justice.*"[8]

Aquinas goes on to emphasize justice not only of one person for another but also for each person toward the whole community of all others. For Aquinas, justice is a cardinal virtue and more significant and crucial in some ways than mercy or fortitude. It is no wonder the Dominicans, the order of which Aquinas was an influential force, have remained focused on justice as central to their understanding of the functions of preaching.[9]

The Dominicans were not alone in their concern for justice, particularly for the poor. The mendicant friars among the Franciscans and the scholars emerging from Franciscan roots sought to establish a just "ecclesiastical economy," and because of their vast preaching efforts, those ideas affected secular reflections on economy as well.[10] That their preaching affected society's perceptions of equity and justice should not be ignored. Imperfect as the results have been, Franciscan attempts to enact the liberating function of preaching for the poor are persistent.

Evangelicals have received well-earned critique for lacking a bent toward justice in society. White Evangelicals in North America were

---

8. Saint Thomas Aquinas, *The Summa Theologica of Saint Thomas Aquinas,* part II, trans. Fathers of the English Dominican Province (London: R&T Washbourne Ltd., 1918), 118 (Question 58, Article 3).

9. See the in-depth work by Francesco Compagnoni and Helen J. Alford, *Preaching Justice: Dominican Contributions to Social Ethics in the Twentieth Century* (Dublin, Ireland: Dominican Publications, 2007), as well as *Preaching Justice Volume II—Contributions of Dominican Sisters to Social Ethics in the Twentieth Century* (Dublin, Ireland: Dominican Publications, 2016).

10. S. Todd Lowry, Barry Lewis, and John Gordon, *Ancient and Medieval Economic Ideas and Concepts of Social Justice* (Leiden, Netherlands: Brill Publications, 1998), 361–67.

not on the front line of the civil rights movement. In general, they were opposed. In the twenty-first century, Evangelicals have only begun to fully face this critique. Donald Dayton's great work *Discovering an Evangelical Heritage* outlines the original justice-oriented nature of the movements of evangelicalism, particularly in the holiness traditions.[11] Store-front missions were attempts not only to theorize about justice but also to systemically enact it. Movements of ministry to and with the poor rooted in the Wesleyan-Methodist revival in England and the popularization of it by Calvinists such as George Whitefield continued into the 1900s.

The history is mixed both for actions and for preaching however. Wesleyan-Methodists, now considered Evangelicals, split from the Methodist mainline church after a great struggle to enact abolitionist ideals. Luther Lee, cofounder of the Wesleyan-Methodists, preached the ordination sermon for Antoinette Brown, making Evangelicals the first to ordain a woman in North America. Brown did not receive the welcome in the average churches in that tradition that she was offered by the leadership, however. She was employed by a Congregationalist church and ultimately became Unitarian.

The socially oriented origins of the Free Methodists or the Salvation Army register that evangelically-minded movements have not always shunned preaching justice. Preachers in evangelical circles in the early 1900s preached against ornate church buildings or "Sunday dress." Simple buildings not only allowed more money to be used to help the poor but also helped poor parishioners feel the church was a place they belonged. Preachers would regularly wear their oldest suits to preach, so that the poor might not feel out of place. Though legalistic applications of the social experiment of prohibition were problematic, Evangelical preachers proposed temperance for social justice–oriented reasons: it prevented the abuse of women that was rampant in alcoholic homes, and it freed money spent on alcohol for the service to the poor.

William Seymour, considered by many to be the founder of Pentecostalism, was trained under these Evangelical holiness preachers. Martin Wells Knapp trained William Seymour in a spirit-focused theology

---

11.   Donald Dayton, *Discovering an Evangelical Heritage*, 1st ed. (New York: Harper & Row, 1976).

of sanctification though the surrounding community did not want Seymour educated in theology. He took the doctrine of the "filling of the heart with love" with him to California and the Azusa Street Revival. Contrary to the eventual position of white Pentecostalism, William Seymour came to believe racial reconciliation was the best determinant of whether or not the Spirit has done its work.[12] Love through racial reconciliation at that time was impossible to fake. His preaching of racial reconciliation made him a national villain to the dominant culture and hero to the marginalized ethnic minorities.

In the 1920s the cooling effects of modernism sent a chill through the ranks of these evangelical-minded Baptists, Wesleyans, Presbyterians, Lutherans, and the like. Great fear that modernist theology would cool the fires of devotion led to the distribution of fundamentalist tracts claiming twelve fundamentals were necessary for vital faith. These tracts were not the primary articulation of evangelical fervor before this point. Instead, since social justice was the primary thing *on which both sides agreed,* it was not inscribed into the distinguishing arguments of fundamentalists. The fight was for doctrine, authority of scripture, literal interpretation of scripture, and the bodily resurrection.

At the same time, liberal theology, having extracted the historicity of the claims of Christianity to transcendant reality, was left primarily with immanent activity—justice for the poor and oppressed. Social gospel movements became the source of meaning and purpose for those who felt that modernism had made faith in miracles, including a resurrection, indefensible. Preachers seemed to be forced to choose sides. There were only two options: concern for authoritative historic doctrine, or concern for social justice and the poor.[13]

For this reason, mainline homileticians and homileticians from minority groups have consistently called for social justice preaching more

---

12. See Harvey Cox, *Fire from Heaven: The Rise of Pentecostal Spirituality and the Reshaping of Religion in the 21st Century* (Cambridge, MA: Da Capo Press, 2009).

13. If the reader has carefully followed the narrative, it is clear that the split between historic doctrine and justice is actually impossible, diluting not only one, but both major branches of theology emerging from the modernist-fundamentalist debate.

than Evangelical, Pentecostal, or Holiness preachers in ensuing decades.[14] In a radical reversal, the very movements that were so heavily involved in justice for the poor and oppressed (even facing opposition from the powers in mainline circles) became opposed to preaching justice. Only in the last twenty years have Evangelical, Pentecostal, and Holiness movements begun to reclaim and refocus attention on something preaching has functioned to do since the Old Testament prophets: free the oppressed and the oppressor from the shackles of injustice. In this sense these movements are returning to their original identity when they use preaching to announce freedom for the captives.

How Does Preaching "Free" the World?

The freeing function of preaching is *the attempt to liberate a community of faith from delusions and systems of injustice so that the world might be a place of equity for all people groups*. The first component of this definition that needs exploration is the notion of delusion. There is a deceptive nature to injustice. It blinds and encourages blindness for those who are in power by rewarding the powerful for their involvement in injustice. Bribery is one concrete and simple example for this. In both simple and complex ways the powerful receive rewards for cooperating with a system of injustice. Injustice both blinds the powerful, on the one hand, and punishes vision for those who are powerless, on the other hand. The powerless, or less powerful, are punished for any clarity of vision for a more just society. From the less aggressive forms of verbal taunting or debate, to the more aggressive forms of termination of employment, social isolation, imprisonment, and hate crimes societies often seek to punish any who see and name injustice. Those who pretend to be blind, who remain silent, are rewarded by being left alone to find the best life they can

---

14.   A complete review of all the books on preaching over the last century focused on preaching justice is impossible for such a short work. Some have already been noted above. Christine Smith's *Preaching Justice, Ethnic and Cultural Perspectives* (Eugene, OR: Wipf and Stock, 2008), Justo L. González and Catherine Gunsalus González's *Liberation Preaching: The Pulpit and the Oppressed* (Nashville: Abingdon Press, 1980), Charles Campbell's *The Word before the Powers*, Walter Brueggemann's *The Practice of the Prophetic Imagination: Preaching an Emancipating Word* (Minneapolis: Fortress Press, 2012), Marvin McMickle's *Where Have All the Prophet's Gone?* and Leonora Tubbs Tisdale's *Prophetic Preaching: A Pastoral Approach* (Louisville, KY: Westminster John Knox Press, 2010) certainly make the short list.

within the structures society has created. As a result, preaching that frees must free both the powerful and the powerless from the deluded blindness of cultural myths.

Most whites in North America, for example, still remain unaware of the inequitable practices of security and police forces. The vast majority of whites have never been asked, "What are you doing in this neighborhood?" as a matter of routine traffic stopping. They remain deluded to believe that society is equally welcoming for all people groups. Black Nihilism is equally problematic. A certain blindness to hope accosts people who are perpetually followed in retail stores, stopped in traffic, stared at in public, unequally sentenced, or shot in the back when they flee out of fear. A sense of despair can overcome any vision of a more just future, leaving some African Americans devoid of any further energy to resist. Latino/a communities sometimes express a parallel Catholic fatalism—"nothing good can happen so enjoy life as much as you can, and go to the priest for absolution."[15] The result often is a lack of any culture of resistance or protest. While this is only the briefest of glances at a central issue of injustice and racism, it demonstrates the need for the removal of delusion for both the powerful and the powerless and those who experience mixed locations of power and powerlessness.

The second component of this definition that requires at least a brief explanation is the phrase *systems of injustice*. In some developing-world countries the existence of what many call "structural evil" is such an obvious everyday fact that speaking of systems of injustice raises no eyebrows among Evangelicals, Pentecostals, extensions of "mainline" churches, Catholics, or any other tradition. It is a given fact. However, preaching against it can trigger seriously detrimental results for the people of the church.

Systems-based thinking undercuts any notion that individual decisions and behavior choices can completely change the system. Societal structures and systems sustain themselves in many ways and actively

---

15. This is merely a paraphrase of a common cultural expression. For more specific guidance on *fatalismo* see Patricia Arredondo, Maritza Gallardo-Cooper, Edward A. Delgado-Romero, and Angela L. Zapata, *Culturally Responsive Counseling With Latinas/os* (Alexandria, VA: American Counseling Association, 2014), esp. 189–91.

punish those who seek to change them. Rather than simply preaching on "issues," truly freeing preaching speaks to "systems." Issues sermons (e.g., homelessness or racism) often lead to decisional ethics, leaving people under the delusion that their minor decisions can affect systemic change. "Decide this, do that, take these three steps." Systems sermons call for a way of life that is built upon nonviolent resistance and liberating practices that become natural ways of life. In this way, liberating preaching is not truly liberating unless it forms new ways of being, valuing, protesting, and resisting in community. It either promotes contextual virtues in the listeners, or it falls short of true freedom. This need for contextual virtues in the listener serves as a reminder that every preaching function requires an attendant contextual virtue in the preacher. We offer what we have.

The liberating function of preaching is best accomplished through preachers who demonstrate a virtuous attendance to justice and a courageous ability to announce it in their preaching life across time and diverse contexts. Some homileticians would argue that every sermon should "preach justice."[16] In other words, the liberating function has been lifted to the level of overarching aim. Every sermon should be aware of issues of justice and seek to ensure that its words do not entrench injustice. Yet justice does not have to be the primary focus of every sermon to do so. A balanced view of pastoral and prophetic concerns is more likely to create lasting change.[17] Other homileticians wish to reserve liberation language only for those from oppressed people groups and use redemption language for privileged people whose lives are held captive by unjust structures, but benefit from them. While this avoids a paternalism that can come from preaching "other people's liberation" and not our own, it confuses the saving and freeing functions of preaching.[18]

---

16. Smith, *Preaching Justice, Ethnic and Cultural Perspectives*. This compendium of essays holds justice as the primary aim of preaching from beginning to end.

17. This is Tisdale's view in *Prophetic Preaching*.

18. See González and González, *Preaching Liberation*. In scripture, redemption language is a metaphor borrowed from unjust societal structures (slavery) but directed toward psychological and spiritual realities (saving, reconciliation with God, forgiveness of the debt of sins, and so forth).

Courageous Justice among the Other Contextual Virtues

Given the above analysis of preaching, the contextual virtue required for the preacher to participate in the liberating function of preaching can be described as *courageous justice*. It is not enough for a preacher to have an intellectual sense of what is just and right and fair in particular cases. That sort of single-case awareness is better than a lack of any justice orientation since it is difficult to understand justice in any other way than from the bottom up, case by case. However, it is also possible to see particular cases of injustice and turn a blind eye. If the reason for turning a blind eye is a lack of concern, compassionate empathy is likely the missing quality. If, however, the eye sees clearly and concern is present, fear may be the reason preachers only walk away saddened. Courage is what is required.

Modifying the virtue of justice with the adjective *courageous* keeps us from engaging in intellectual discussions and self-righteous head nodding without any personal/communal risk or personal/communal action. The virtue of courageous justice does not simply involve recognition of injustice, or anger at injustice. Action is required. This leads to the following definition:

> Courageous justice is *the habitual valuing of equity for all people groups leading to increasing personal risk-taking on the behalf of others.*

Courageous justice swims upstream against the natural human tendency toward self-preservation in order to embody love in the arena of intergroup relations and societal structures. The current of human self-interest presses humans to protect personal interests and the personal interests of those most like them (which is a preservation of self). People tend to love *selective* mercy and do *occasional* justice.

Human beings particularly love mercy when we, or someone we love, needs it; and do justice when we, or someone we love, is deprived of it. We do not love mercy so easily when someone with whom we compete is in need of grace. Nor do we typically do justice when someone whom we despise is deprived of it. The virtue of courageous justice is greater to the degree that it is consistent across contexts of convenience or inconvenience, affinity or opposition, reward or retaliation.

The line of division between courageous justice and the other contextual virtues for preaching cannot be easily drawn. Christian virtue theory has always claimed that virtue is unitary with love as the unifying virtue. Humility, empathy, wisdom, and justice are all ways of describing different aspects of love as love finds expression in situ. The interrelationship is not confused, however. There is a certain flow of logic to the movement through the contextual virtues for preaching. Once courageous justice is added to the mix, the other three have even more helpful clarity than before. See appendix C for an illustration of the virtues in the context of the aim and functions of preaching.

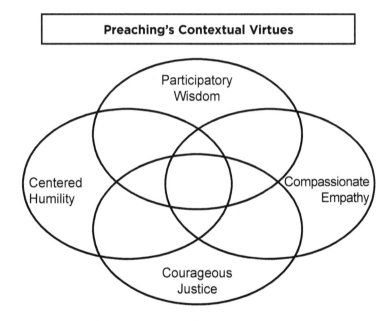

Centered humility maintains the self and validates the perspective of the normally marginalized preacher, while also questioning self-sufficiency of preachers whose social location lends itself to privileged pride. This centered humility also enables the preacher seeking to acquire courageous justice the core attitude and intention necessary to do so: a deeply habitual recognition of need for the perspectives of others. How else can we know justice? Without the powerful humbly seeking others' perspectives and the oppressed owning and expressing their own perspectives, we will not be able to discern justice. Anyone who thinks the expression of experiences of injustice is not humbling has most likely never experienced injustice to any great degree.

Compassionate empathy moves from the centered self, outward in a reverse of the classical definition of sin (curved in on oneself). The outward movement of understanding—and care—for others' real suffering helps the preacher actively "shatter deliberate ignorance and willful blindness" as Cornel West so poignantly phrased it.[19] This shattering must first and foremost happen for the preacher. Without compassionate empathy others' mountains will always be molehills and others' laments only signs of ingratitude.

With humility and empathy, the stories of others work to rupture the preacher's self-contained, self-promoting ideologies. A world we cannot love confronts us as real, for those we love are wounded by it. This empathy gives the preacher seeking courageous justice a core attitude and intention necessary to do so: the embrace of diverse others' experiences *with concern* to alleviate their suffering and enable their good.[20] On the flip side, compassionate empathy can often lead us only to try to make people feel better in our preaching. As James Harris warns, "Too often the preacher makes... people feel content with their sins and at peace with the world, rather than forcing them to become uncomfortable and dissatisfied with the inequities and injustices that we observe, participate in, and often, create."[21] In preaching, there is a time for comforting the upset. There is also a time for upsetting the comfortable.

Participatory wisdom presses the preacher to engage in the content of the claims of God upon her soul. Unless the preacher participates in the claims of scripture in the presence of a moving Spirit to "love mercy and

---

19. Cornel West, *Democracy Matters* (New York: Penguin Books, 2004), 115.

20. Whereas compassionate empathy is directed toward individuals, courageous justice is most often directed toward people groups. Whereas compassionate empathy motivates a preacher to alleviate suffering, courageous justice motivates a preacher to resist injustice or inequity. Many preachers give only individualistic "applications" in sermons when the text requires a more communal and systemic reaction to injustice.

21. James H. Harris, *Preaching Liberation* (Minneapolis: Fortress Press, 1995), 56.

do justice" the preacher cannot fully understand the good news for the poor or freedom for the captives. It is not easy to do justice. The steps for Christian justice in the face of a particular instance of injustice may be articulated simply, but not lived easily. Further, resisting injustice in one instance does not free the world from unjust systems. Wisdom is required to discern what actions will best help dismantle unjust systems and construct equitable ones. Participatory wisdom then gives the preacher the necessary attitude and intention for the acquiring of courageous justice: experiential understanding resulting from the holistic engagement of the preacher over time with justice in diverse contexts of life.

Sketching the Preacher of Courageous Justice

What does courageous justice look like in the preacher and in the preaching life? First of all, a courageously just preacher *sees what "can be" just as clearly as "what is."* Leonora Tubbs Tisdale in *Prophetic Preaching* calls these two poles of prophetic preaching the "criticizing" (what is) and the "energizing" (can be) poles.[22] The prophetic preacher refuses to see her role as simply the caretaker of a tradition, the maintainer of what has been, or the priest of an unjust kingdom. The prophet refuses to accept *what is* in light of her vision of what *can be.*

Second, a preacher who exhibits courageous justice *takes the internal risk of seeking truth and equity.* A courageously just preacher must be well studied and informed on an issue before speaking. Yet study cannot merely be a search for support of previously held positions. If the positions return, so be it; if the positions must be sacrificed, so be it. It is one of the most troubling things imaginable to put your deeply held beliefs at risk. This is often more fear inducing than publicly naming injustices and calling for justice on those positions already held. Announcing what you already believe only risks rejection by people with whom you disagree. When a preacher puts his beliefs up for debate, he or she risks losing some part of his or herself, and risks the rejection of those with whom he or she

---

22. Tisdale, *Prophetic Preaching*, 10.

used to agree, it is a great risk, for these are friends, family, and church leaders whose opinions the preacher cherishes. Yet preachers cannot preach justice without taking that risk. The prior risk to public justice is the risk of personal and communal rejection. This of course implies, much time spent in study, reflection, discussion, and prayer. If it is done well, many of those close to the preacher are slowly brought into the journey with her. Often the first act of prophetic proclamation happens in small groups, leadership circles, coffee klatches, and discipleship meetings long before a word enters the pulpit.

Third, a preacher who exhibits courageous justice *publicly denounces an evil in society and announces a strategy for equitable change.* This is the risk of justice. The marginalized preacher risks great persecution or injustice in retaliation when she names evil and proclaims a better way. The privileged preacher speaks against her own complicit way of life on behalf of marginalized groups. In doing so she risks joining the marginalized by loss of power, privilege, and status—even the loss of life along with the persecuted.[23] Preachers cannot pretend to hope that seeking others' freedom will not enrage those who benefit from their captivity. A preacher announcing justice risks painful rejection, lowered church attendance, loss of friendships, removal of ordination, and in some cases the loss of life.

The preacher who engages acts of justice may also come face to face with "the powers and principalities" that structurally and persistently oppose all attempts to bring equity to a world built for the rich, privileged, and violent. In North America where I live, we fear a day when the preacher of courageous justice has to duck beneath the pulpit because of gunfire yet again. If we have been paying attention, that day has already returned (if it ever left). For ministry brothers and sisters in many countries around the world, violence because of the name of Christ is a daily reality. For Jesus, liberating preaching led to a cross. In Paul's day, freeing the people of God led to stoning, flogging, lashing, and imprisonment

---

23. Every pastor has to deal with the tension of how much of her convictions to reveal how soon so as to help people move toward justice. Movements toward justice are often like pulling cars with exercise bands. There must be enough bands put into tension before bands can carry the load without breaking. Often when the bands of unity break, a lash back occurs leaving the church more entrenched in injustice as a result. Wisdom knows the right time and right procedure. Still, if the procedure is not moving forward, it is unjust.

among other things. Eventually, it led to death. "Woe to you when all speak well of you," our Lord warns (Luke 6:26, NRSV).

For Reflection

1. Are there any issues of justice that you have avoided studying or discussing in order to avoid making a decision? Force yourself to write down the issues you have avoided.

2. This chapter references the risk of justice in a summary way. What specific risks cause the preacher to back away from courageous justice and therefore stunt the liberating power of the pulpit?

3. Unbounded freedom is no freedom at all. We are not only freed from, Karl Barth taught us, but free for. How can a preacher bind the freeing power of preaching to the gospel so as to avoid lawlessness, doctrinal chaos, or loss of good news?

4. Who are your diverse models for courageous justice in preaching? Make a short list and reflect on their qualities.

5. Seeing the pressing issues of justice for bygone eras is much easier than seeing our own time. What are the most pressing issues of justice in this era that you discern? Discuss your list with someone of significant difference from you. How does discussing an issue with someone of significant difference help to round out your views of justice?

CHAPTER 5
Practicing a Christian Life

The morning was slipping away and sermon preparation was on my mind.[1] The text was chosen and read, and study had begun. Then, the call came to go to the hospital. It was a knee (a knee!). "This is not an issue of life and death," I caught myself thinking. Why should I go to the hospital and forsake the sermon when it is only a knee? I drove to the hospital with a smoldering resentment in my heart. It had been an unusually heavy pastoral season in the absence of other pastors who left for other ministry appointments. I needed to find a way to pull a sermon together. Walking up to the room, I felt the cold fear in the hallways of the surgery wing. I saw it, like frozen steel in the eyes of my parishioner. He was terrified. I heard it in the voice of his wife as she described the surgery's brutality. They shared much, I mostly listened, and we prayed briefly.

Walking back to the car the legitimate worry in my friends' lives hung in front of my mind like a compelling piece of art. I had been so busy searching for a good sermon I resented the opportunity to live a good life. The ride home was a prayerful ride with repentant requests for a heart of love to return. It seemed love was already returning. The next hour in the office was full of improvisational attempts to verbally and visually rewrite the sermon to include legitimate fear, legitimate worry, and the reality of uncertainty in life. The sermon never mentioned the hospital, never told the story of their fear, but it pulsed with the emotion and faith of that pre-surgery worship moment.

---

1. See chapter 6 for reasons why starting Sunday's sermon study on Monday is detrimental to the preaching life.

This is a question preachers would benefit from asking regularly, "Which am I seeking most: a good life or a good sermon?"[2] Ministers often miss living a good life because we are too focused on finding a good sermon. Hospital visits were not the only activity I was initially frustrated with in that early season. Discipleship meetings with prisoners, sharing at the local mission, nursing home visitations, and a meeting with a mentally challenged congregant all tempted me to grumble, "Now how do I get a sermon together for Sunday?" The front-end negativity regularly gave way to after-the-fact gratitude. The lesson in the first few years of ministry was clear. Those moments of presence with others were deeply meaningful ministry in and of themselves, but they were also more than that. They invalidated previously held beliefs that were not humble, empathetic, wise, or just. Moreover, they inspired sermons I never would have thought of otherwise. They were not direct sermon material. Those moments rarely should be, and only years later with permission. Yet they were the tools used by the Spirit to begin forming the contextual attentiveness I was lacking.

Sunday is coming. This is true. Still, the more near-sighted preachers become in their focus on the next sermon, the longer they will remain in a hand-to-mouth pattern for preaching preparation. A deeply Christian way of life, when practiced well, yields sermons with much greater depth and ease. A deeply Christian way of life also prevents us from many sermonic sins we will only regret later.

So far, we have explored the preacher's longing (the aim), doing (the functions), and being (contextual virtues). The challenge of the person of the preacher is now clearly in view: How does a preacher who feels more prideful/shameful than humble, more unaware than empathetic, more naive or foolish than wise, or more selfish than just gain these virtues? Perhaps more important, how does the preacher who lacks these qualities, but does not realize it, gain them over time? The concern is strengthened when we see the ghosts of legalism, moralism, pietism, and Pelagianism hanging in the shadows. Do we make ourselves virtuous or does God?

---

2. There is danger in asking this question. Some will automatically replace "good life" with "perfect life" and therefore miss the grace in the question.

If it is through our own effort (even through practices) then we have resurrected Pelagian heresy. If it is through God and God alone regardless of our efforts, then other shadows fall. We are involved somehow.

The means of grace have long been the answer to these fears. Though the means of grace can be called practices, they are not merely things humans do. Christian practices are places God invites us to be so that Spirit(ual) formation can be received as grace not works.[3] Practices do not need to turn the grace of God into a vending machine. Spirit(ual) practices are not merely levers and switches that automate the grace of God like grace dispensers. The Spirit of God is the primary agent in the spiritual formation of the preacher. The means of grace are merely practices Christians believe God has ordained to be loci of the Spirit's presence, mercy, and transformative work. We go to the Christian practices and wait for God to grace us in ways we anticipate but would not expect. Christian practices are places in which we feel called to abide, trusting God will meet us *there*.

For this reason, this chapter forms the backbone of this book. It is the structure of life that holds all of the rest together. It will be tempting to quickly move on from this chapter to more truly homiletical, practical concerns. However, without a Christian life funded by joining in the life of God, the preaching life will always be misconstrued and less than good news.

This view of Christian practices emerges best from a theology of grace intertwining God's command and God's promise within the call of Christ. The biblical Christ repeatedly says, "Follow me," in the initial call to discipleship. This call is both command and promise in the single phrase. The text makes the authority of Christ clear. To stay is to disobey the One to whom all authority is given. The promise of Christ is also clear. If the disciple follows Christ, necessarily the disciple is in the presence of Christ. This intertwining of command and promise is present in the sending of the disciples as well. "Go and make disciples" is the command and

---

3. Offsetting *Spirit* with the parenthetical *(ual)* highlights the agency of God in what is sometimes seen as a-personal "formation." The use of *Spirit(ual)* was inspired by Luke Powery's work on preaching and African American spirituals, *Dem Dry Bones: Preaching, Death, and Hope* (Minneapolis: Fortress Press, 2012). Luke Powery discusses the "Spirit(ual)" side of preaching keeping the Spirit as separate to highlight God's active role in the preaching process.

includes all other commands "teaching them to obey everything that I've commanded you." Yet the promise is clear, "Look, I myself will be with you every day until the end of this present age" (Matt 28:19-20).[4] God's command is always interwoven with a gracious promise—the promise of divine presence.

Wesleyan and Reformed Theologies of Christian Practices

The Wesleyan movement of the seventeenth and eighteenth centuries was so characterized by its spiritual formation through practices that it is what the movement became known by: the "methods" of the Methodists.[5] Wesley saw his practice-centered ecclesiology as a reclaiming movement, reinstating a new version of the history of Christian life across the ages. His continuation of the "middle way" tradition of Anglicanism brings together threads of Catholicism, Orthodoxy, and broader Protestant thought and life.

Craig Dykstra and Dorothy C. Bass have led the way in articulating means of grace for current English-speaking Christian communities particularly in North America. Dykstra and Bass operate primarily from a Reformed/Lutheran theological perspective.[6] When Wesley's theology of Christian practices is placed into conversation with Dykstra and Bass both theologies are strengthened. The weaknesses of each are met with the strength of the other. This section will briefly engage both in an attempt

---

4. Regarding the CEB translation of Matthew 28:19-20: Though the CEB version may not be as familiar to many, the translation is much closer to the meaning of the Greek. It captures the emphatic use of *I* along with the first-person singular verb, highlights the daily nature of the promise of presence (*tas hemeras*), and makes more clear the meaning of *synteleia*, which indicates culmination/completion, not merely an "end."

5. The derisive colloquial label was "Methodies" or worse, "blue tract Methodies," whose evangelistic enthusiasm was combined with their methodological discipline in ways that offended normal English sensibilities.

6. Dykstra is an ordained minister in the PC (USA), and Bass is a scholar and pastor within the Evangelical Lutheran Church in America. Both worked closely with the Valparaiso Project, which was directed at the formation of faith through Christian practices. The ELCA is in full communion with the PC (USA), RCA, and UCC, demonstrating the shared theological and ecclesial commitments uniting their faith perspectives.

to come to a stronger position for Christian practices as formative for the preaching life. Five points of mutual agreement are outlined below between Reformed and Wesleyan-Arminian perspectives on a theology of Christian practices.

First and foremost, Dykstra asserts it is God's gracious activity that makes the practices of the life of faith truly formative Christian practices. The practices are not merely something Christians do to be formed in virtues of the "Christian" life they have been enculturated to pursue.[7] Both Dykstra and Bass's Reformed views and the Wesleyan view outlined below emphasize God as supremely involved in Christian practices. As Dykstra states it, "By active participation in practices that are central to the historical life of the community of faith, we place ourselves in the kind of situation in which we know God accomplishes the work of grace."[8] Christian practices are "outward means of grace," not merely socially constructed practices.[9] Here Dykstra brings this discussion of Christian practices to a place where MacIntyre could not. Practices through which God actively mediates grace to the being-saved community are central to Christian faith.[10]

Dykstra divides the activity of God in relation to formative Christian practices into three interrelated characteristics: promise, presence, and place.[11] First, formative Christian practices carry with them the characteristic of *promise* because God has promised to use these particular practices as means of grace. Further, we know these to be means of grace

---

7. In this way, Christian formative practices cannot be understood solely in the way all practices are understood by Alasdair MacIntyre. Mastery of these practices through pursuit of excellence and focus on the internal goods of these practices while pursuing the ultimate aim of the practices misses the central claim of Christian practices: God's grace.

8. Dykstra, *Growing in the Life of Faith*, (Louisville, KY: Westminster John Knox Press, 2005), 42. Dykstra gives his definition of practices as "things Christian people do together over time to address fundamental human needs in response to and in light of God's active presence for the life of the world (in Jesus Christ)." See also Dykstra and Bass, "A Theological Understanding of Christian Practices," in *Practicing Theology: Beliefs and Practices in Christian Life*, ed. Miroslav Volf and Dorothy C. Bass (Grand Rapids, MI: William B. Eerdmans, 2001), 18. There is a parenthetical correction from note 3 on p. 18.

9. Dykstra, *Growing in the Life of Faith*, 41–42.

10. As will be seen more clearly below through the category of practices of compassion, this grace is given to the being-saved community for the sake of the world.

11. These are not Dykstra's stated structures. Rather they are theological themes that run throughout the work and are consistently maintained.

because one of the things the Bible does for us "is to render a promise."[12] This promise emerges from the character of the nature of God who is "a God of promise who can be depended on to keep promises."[13] Further, to live faithfully in relationship to this God is to live as one who has heard, believed, and now "responds to those promises."[14] Following the Larger Catechism of the Presbyterian Church, Dykstra names the particular means of grace that are the recipients of God's promise as "ordinances" of Christ.[15] Among these ordinances three rise beyond others: "the Word, sacraments, and prayer."[16] In and through these, God promises to bestow life-transforming grace.

The concept of promise contains within it the second characteristic of Dykstra's Christian practices: presence. The promise of God is not that these practices will automate the grace of God, as though the grace of God is functionally identical with the practices. Rather, *the promise is God will be there.* Specifically, Christ will be present to us through the activity of the Spirit. This leads Dykstra to clarify writing, "The practices of faith are not ultimately our own practices but rather habitations of the Spirit, in the midst of which we are invited to participate in the practices of God."[17]

By the phrase *habitations of the Spirit* Dykstra intends to imply the third characteristic of God's agency in Christian practices: *place.* Rather than conceiving of practices as things we do, they are places to which we go. More important, they are places in which God chooses to dwell through the Spirit, loci of God's gracious presence. This language remains relatively consistent throughout *Growing in the Life of Faith* in which Dykstra repeatedly emphasizes that these are "human places" where we find "God made present."[18] Here our conception of practices is shifted

---

12. Dykstra, *Growing in the Life of Faith,* 59. See also Jürgen Moltmann, *Theology of Hope: On the Ground and the Implications of a Christian Eschatology* (New York: Harper & Row, 1967); Christopher Morse, *The Logic of Promise in Moltmann's Theology* (Philadelphia: Fortress Press, 1979); James F. Kay, *Preaching and Theology* (St. Louis: Chalice Press, 2007), 120–25.

13. Dykstra, *Growing in the Life of Faith,* 59.

14. Ibid., 59.

15. Ibid., 52.

16. Ibid.

17. Ibid., 78.

18. Ibid., 43. See also 6, 10, 21, 38–39, 47, and 53.

from activities to places, and from mere doing to faithful dwelling.[19] We live in Christian practices the way a community lives within a town.

This shift from doing to dwelling offers two benefits to our understanding of practices for the life of preaching. First, dwelling connotes that practices form a place and way of living and as such are not merely additions to another way of life. Second, focus on dwelling rather than doing helps avoid the mechanization of God's grace. Participation in the practices does not force God's hand or automate the dispensing of something called grace.[20] The seeking Christian repeatedly goes where God has commanded her to go and waits for the Spirit to do in God's own time and choosing what God has promised to do.

A fourth claim Dykstra makes that Wesleyan theology affirms is the interconnected and interdependent nature of formative Christian practices. Dykstra asserts that "no one practice is the key to faith and the life of faith."[21] Instead, they enable one another, overlap with one another, and prompt one another in the way salty food calls for water. For example, the practices of Christian worship naturally send believers out into intentional engagement with practices of compassion and mercy for the world. They send as well as sustain, inform, and equip.

Fifth, this theological reading of Christian practices leads Dykstra to define the ways of being they require: "receptivity and responsiveness."[22] For Dykstra receptivity is required since it is primarily God who is acting as the initiating, sustaining, and transforming agent. Mastering the technique of an activity alone is a "forceful striving" that is inappropriate for formative Christian practices.[23] Responsiveness indicates that God invites

---

19. It will be seen in the section below that this insight is not unique to Dykstra but is woven throughout Christianity's theological traditions surrounding Christian practices.

20. Shirley C. Guthrie Jr., *Christian Doctrine* (Atlanta: John Knox Press, 1968), 299–300. "If new life is a gift of the Holy Spirit, we cannot give it to ourselves....We have been told who he is, and where and how he is promised. Although we cannot control his coming and going, we can at least place ourselves in the kind of situation in which we know he accomplishes his work (p. 311)."

21. Dykstra, *Growing in the Life of Faith*, 45.

22. Ibid., 76. See also Craig Dykstra and Dorothy Bass, "A Theological Understanding of Christian Practices" in Volf, *Practicing Theology*, 13–32. Here Dykstra and Bass maintain these two stances as the primary description of human faithfulness.

23. Dykstra, *Growing in the Life of Faith*, 76.

us to participate in these practices in a way that is congruent with God's own activity in the nature of response rather than initiation.[24]

Dykstra's Reformed perspective and a Wesleyan perspective have significant consonance with each other. The significant agreement might be summarized in these five mutual claims: (1) God promises to be graciously active *through* these practices. (2) God's promise to be active includes the promise to be present *in* formative Christian practices. (3) Practices are then not primarily doings but *dwellings where we live* in anticipation of God's presence. (4) Christian practices are interconnected and interdependent. (5) Christians' faithful participation in Christian practices is characterized by receptivity and responsiveness to God's active presence.

A Wesleyan theology of Christian practices offers three strengthening components to the Reformed/Lutheran views outlined above. The above discussion without modification has three weaknesses for the preacher seeking a life of faith formed by Christian practices: a loss of divine command, a loose or vaguely defined set of practices, and a division between promise (grace) and obedience (law). Wesleyan theology benefits from the emphases of the Reformed/Lutheran views particularly in the renewed emphases on promise over against duty, presence over against discipline, and place over against performance. Wesleyan theology strengthens the Reformed/Lutheran view by regaining the divine command, clearly defining the practices, and reuniting promise and obedience.

First, the emphasis on the gracious promise of God to be present in the central practices (primarily the sacraments) of the church is helpful and inspiring. However, except for in a few cases, Dykstra's emphasis on gracious promise leaves out the sovereignty of command the language of "ordinances" traditionally contains. His lists of practices are unhinged from the commands of the biblical Christ and emerge from the community's life. Without a measure or normative guide, Christian communal life loses its defining clarity.

---

24. Dykstra seeks to critically appropriate the theory of practices that MacIntyre provides by shifting its central focus away from human standards, human excellence, and human striving.

It is broadly accepted, with some debate about terms, that Wesley's construal of his tradition's orienting theological concept can be described as "responsible grace."[25] Grace is the first and foremost word. Response is the first human portion of this concept. God's grace is always acting, always sovereign, always prior to human action.[26] God in Christ is reconciling the world, and this reconciling grace precedes all Christians in all acts, not only the preacher. We respond to what God is already doing rather than act so that God might respond. As a result, not only do we respond to God's grace but also God's grace enables us to respond. Since we have been made able to respond through the internal, mysterious, active work of the Spirit of love, we are now *response*-able and *responsible* to love. And what is the vehicle for God's filling of our hearts with love? The means of grace, or Christian practices.

A Wesleyan view of practices claims particular means of grace have been proclaimed as the "ordinary channels whereby [God] might convey...preventing, justifying, or sanctifying grace."[27] The ordinances bear with them the character of command, to which we are responsible only due to God's gracious promise and God's enabling grace. A few examples will be sufficient to recall commands to mind: the Christ of Scripture commands us to "do this in remembrance of me," "repent and be baptized," and "watch and pray."[28] The ordinances of Christ are ordained as promises, but the promises bear with them a directive. It is not a burdensome command, but a well-fitting yoke that connects the

---

25. Randy Maddox, *Responsible Grace: John Wesley's Practical Theology* (Nashville: Kingswood Books, 1994), 17–19. Maddox modifies this concept from Gerhard Sauter's "orientierender Begriffe" in *Arbeitsweisen Systematishcer Theologie: Eine Anleitung* (Munich: Christian Kaiser, 1976), 157–58. Maddox exchanges Sauter's "concepts" (Begriffe) for concern in order to avoid labeling Wesley as more systematic than he intends and also to imply the meta-conceptual nature of what he labels an orienting concern. See again Maddox's *Responsible Grace* (18).

26. This is of course the doctrine of prevenient grace. God's grace always comes before and enables all human response.

27. John Wesley, "Means of Grace," in *The Works of John Wesley*: vol. 5, 1st Series of Sermons 1–39. Also, see *Life of John Wesley* (Grand Rapids, MI: Zondervan, 1958), 251.

28. See Luke 22:19, Acts 2:38, and Matthew 26:41. I do not mean to imply a literalistic, Biblicist understanding of the ordinances of Scripture as though all imperatives in the Gospels and epistles, even the Old Testament, are to be assumed as universally binding. Some commands, such as "bring me my cloak," cannot be considered literally binding. Neither is the command to Judas to go and do evil quickly a command to follow, simply because Christ uses an imperative.

Christian community to the ongoing promised work of Christ through the Spirit.

Insisting on a dual unity of command and promise for Christian practices is not a minor theological quibble unrelated to preaching. Preachers are as tempted as anyone else to pick and choose from the salad bar of Christian practices to form their own way of life. Adding response-ability and therefore responsibility to the Christian practices aids the preacher. If the minister can accept the command *as* promise, then *discipleship is not something preachers have to create; it is something we may receive.* The preacher is not tempted by the false promise of "freedom" to define our own lives our own ways, pursuing our own happiness through our own means. Preaching discipleship begins with discipleship of the preacher. Yet this is not a moralistic statement, but a promise of a gift. The life shaped by Christian practices is a gift that needs to be unwrapped, but it is not a gift we have to make ourselves.

Each theological tradition emerges from an orienting concern common to the tradition. The orienting concern of Wesleyan theology is *for Christianity to be a self-consistent agent for its unfolding vision of God's good in the world.* Wesley wants to see Christianity deliver on its promises. The root of that promise to him is found in the shaping of a communal way of life that is worshipful in all its days and ways and missional in its outward bent. Preaching had not achieved its historic aim in England by Wesley's estimation.[29] Wesley longed to send a doxological community into the world through the proclamation of the gospel, as have all the great preachers of Christian history. He recognized the shape of life the community took would be the primary determinant of whether or not preaching reached its ultimate aim.

It is from the maintenance of the Wesleyan tradition's orienting concern and concept through Christian practices that the best moments of the Wesleyan tradition emerge. The orienting concept (responsible grace/holy love) led Wesleyans to engage in regular practices of receiving and

---

29. John Wesley, "The Causes of the Inefficacy of Christianity," in *The Works of John Wesley*, vol. 7, Second Series of Sermons Concluded (Grand Rapids, MI: Zondervan, 1959), 281ff. In this sermon Wesley asks, "Why has Christianity done so little good in the world?" The kind nonbeliever outshines the English Christian. This deeply disturbs Wesley and shapes his theological reflection in all avenues including his preaching.

responding to God's grace privately and corporately. Public and private reflection on scripture, individual and corporate prayer, communion, fasting, visiting the imprisoned and the sick, and more led them to convictions about the suffering world the staid church of England did not reach. The orienting concern for Christianity to be a self-consistent agent of God's good in the world is what drove Wesleyans into early adoption of liberating social positions such as abolitionism, ordination of women, and critiques of abused church power.[30]

These practices brought early Wesleyans into empathetic contact with slaves as brothers and sisters, women as called ones of God, and the victims of abuses of power as iconic representations of the face of Christ.[31] The humble submission of their lives to a set of Christian practices led them to gain empathy for the suffering and to learn wise ways of engaging that suffering, and then courageous and just social action eventually occurred.

Three major additions to current Christian practices discussions emerge from this dialogue. First, formative Christian practices come to us, not as options, but as response-abilities. The loss of the third use of the law for Christian practices can do damage to Christianity's ultimate ability to "stick" with them and therefore does damage to Christianity's self-consistency. This is particularly true for those who enjoy relative comfort, wealth, or power. It is difficult enough to get privileged persons to engage justice *when there is a divine command* to appeal to, let alone without one. It is perhaps most important for those in places of relative privilege and power to receive the divine command along with the promise. The rest of the world suffers otherwise.

According to Dykstra, practices are not "duties we undertake to be obedient. Rather, they are patterns of communal action that create openings in our lives where the grace, mercy, and presence of God may be made known to us."[32] This emphasis on grace is commendable. Still, it is not wrong to pursue Christian practices out of obedience. Grace and obedience

---

30. This liberative impulse continued long after Wesley was gone. The Wesleyan-Methodist connection, for example, was founded in 1843 for "the abolition of slavery and against episcopacy" along with issues of labor reform and women's rights. See Lee M. Haines and Paul William Thomas, *An Outline History of the Wesleyan Church*, 6th ed. (Indianapolis, IN: Wesleyan Publishing House, 2005), 39, 66–67.

31. Donald Dayton, *Discovering an Evangelical Heritage* (Peabody, MA: Hendrickson, 1988).

32. Dykstra, *Growing in the Life of Faith*, 66.

are not opposed. Dykstra intends to avoid legalistic self-righteous practices. This is important. The use of *should* and *ought to* and *must* can be replaced with *want, can,* and *will.* Yet the preacher who does not yet "want" to follow Christ's call to live within the Christian practices will be better off if she seeks the desire to practice *while* obeying the call to practice. She should not insist on finding desire before beginning the practice. Our hearts will eventually align with Christ's desire, but first we can only trust the Spirit to make good on the promise and change our hearts *within the practices.*

The second problem is a somewhat vague list of Christian practices throughout Christian practices literature. The Wesleyan tradition has from its beginning held to a very defined set of formative Christian practices conceived as ordinances. These practices for the Methodists would not have been categorized in as broad terms as Dykstra and Bass have in "honoring the body, hospitality, household economics, saying yes and saying no, keeping Sabbath, discernment, testimony, shaping communities, forgiveness, healing, dying well, and singing our lives to God."[33] Certainly, keeping the Sabbath, testimony, forgiveness, and singing our lives to God would ring familiar tones in any Methodist movement. However, for Wesley and the movement he led, practices such as visiting the poor transcended broadly human practices such as "saying yes and saying no."[34] It was clear that "the practice of visitation was directly necessary for developing the sort of compassion that, for Wesley, was the heart of true religion.... [Visitation of the poor] was a means of grace to be ranked alongside private and public prayer or the sacraments themselves."[35] The contextual virtue of compassionate empathy requires the practices of ministry to, with, and among the least of these.

Christian practices then are not merely subsets of larger social practices you might find elsewhere such as household economics or saying *yes* and saying *no.* They are distinctively ordained practices that bear the

---

33. Dykstra and Bass, "A Theological Understanding of Christian Practices," in Volf and Bass, *Practicing Theology,* 19. Here again is a mix of specificity (keeping Sabbath) and rather nondescript vague labels (singing our lives) that could be appropriated in any context or community such as a karaoke bar.

34. Jackson, *Works,* 5:251–53.

35. Theodore W. Jennings Jr. *Good News to the Poor: John Wesley's Evangelical Economics* (Nashville: Abingdon Press, 1990) 54.

character of both promise and command. The early Methodists obeyed the command believing the promise that a way of life formed by means of grace was the best way for a human to live. The structured practices helped them participate in the Spirit's outpouring of love into their hearts. Under Wesley's lead they did so in bands and classes of community and support.[36] Wesley saw these activities as natural outgrowths of the Spirit's work and as, more important, loci of the ongoing work of the Spirit in shaping communities in Christian identity and mission.[37]

These Christian practices are infused with the grace of God by the active presence of the Spirit for calling and enabling the believer toward grace-filled living. Singing spiritual songs, Sabbath-keeping, confessing of sins, participating in communion, face-to-face ministry to the poor, opposing injustice, defending the oppressed, and the like are rooted in the scriptural narratives and viewed as divinely ordained practices. We do not engage in them *merely* to "go on" with our tradition, and to transmit from one generation to the next the values and culture of the past. Christians live within Christian practices with receptivity and responsiveness trusting *God meets us there.*

Practices of Devotion and Practices of Compassion

To offer even greater clarity to practices of the Christian faith, Wesleyan theology offers a twofold scheme for the categorization of the diverse practices of the Christian faith under the headings "works of piety" and "works of mercy." Works of piety are the instituted means of grace that bear with them the character of unending command and focus on the love of God. Works of mercy include both instituted and "prudential" or contextual means of grace that vary across time and place in their

---

36. Dykstra and Bass may leave this under the heading of "shaping communities" in Volf and Bass, *Practicing Theology*, "A Theological Understanding of Christian Practices," 19. There are numerous Christian practices that are part of shaping communities. Wesley's bands and classes were an attempt to contextually concretize the "shaping of communities" through certain specific identifiable practices: confession, corporate prayer, giving to those in need, communal study of scripture, and so forth.

37. For a useful description of Wesley's formation of communal life through structured practices, see Rupert E. Davies, ed., *The Works of John Wesley*, vol. 9, "The Methodist Societies: History, Nature, and Design" (Nashville: Abingdon Press, 1989), 8–29.

particulars. Though they vary contextually, they still bear with them the character of command as a whole and focus on loving neighbor.[38]

For example, feeding the hungry is an ordinance instituted by Christ in Matthew 25. It is a work of mercy. The particular way a community decides to be committed to this work of mercy (such as community gardens or food pantries) is a prudential means. The Christ of Scripture does not command specific and concrete methods of structuring works of mercy. He does command the practice of works of mercy in general.[39]

Both works of mercy and works of piety are divided by Wesley into individual and communal elements. The communal works of piety included communion, baptism, community or "Christian conferencing," public testimony, corporate song, and the reading and proclamation of scriptures.[40] The works of piety in the individual realm would include private prayer, fasting, searching the scriptures, and even healthy living. The works of mercy that were focused on individual needs would include visiting the sick, visiting the imprisoned, feeding and clothing those in need (in person if at all possible), as well as diligent earning and saving for the sake of giving.[41] The works of mercy focused on communal needs included all prudential means of seeking justice for the oppressed through actions such as active opposition to the institution of slavery.

Unfortunately, "works" language carries with it both negative connotations (from the Pauline corpus) and positive connotations (from the epistle of James). Here practice theory offers new language bereft of

---

38. Kevin Twain Lowery, *Salvaging Wesley's Agenda: A New Paradigm for Wesleyan Virtue Ethics*, Princeton Theological Monograph Series, 86 (Eugene, OR: Pickwick, 2008), 128. Prudential means are not instituted in scripture individually but are discerned as helpful for the pursuit of the life of love by a particular community like the Methodist movement. The prudential means are primarily contextually discerned ways of concretely living out the more general commands of Christ. These are also subject to change whenever circumstances or common sense dictate the change.

39. A useful summary of these practices as understood in the early Methodist movement can be found in William James Abraham and James E. Kirby, *Oxford Handbook on Methodist Studies* (Oxford: Oxford University Press, 2009), 281–84.

40. This list is from the perspective of the leaders of worship. From the congregation or participants perspective, the last two would read: "hearing the scriptures [read or expounded]."

41. Wesley states the necessity for in-person practice of mercy this way: "Suppose you could give the same relief to the sick by another, you could not reap the same advantage to yourself. You could not gain that increase in lowliness, in patience, in tenderness of spirit, in sympathy with the afflicted, which you might have gained if you had assisted them in person" ("On Visiting the Sick," in *Sermons on Several Occasions*, ed. T. Jackson [London: J. Kershaw, 1825], 524).

the anxious striving embedded in Wesleyan terms such as *works* or *piety*. Works of piety are better termed *practices of devotion*. Works of mercy can be named *practices of compassion*.[42] Practices of devotion and practices of compassion each include both individual and communal spheres. When these categories are kept in view, they help Christians ensure participation in the entire web of Christian practices over time. There are practices of devotion that are individual, and those that are communal. There are practices of compassion that are done for individuals, and those that are pursued for a community.

Many of these practices are not engaged in daily (even weekly), and none of them need to be performed perfectly. None of these practices are required for God's grace, yet all of these practices come with the promise of grace. Appendix D highlights the Christian practices in a summary way allowing for at-a-glance personal reflection. Remember, *the aim of Christian practices is not to perfect performance, but to practice the presence of God.* Remaining in Christ through these means of grace shapes the preacher into the life of Christ.

Preaching can also be best understood when it is embedded within this diverse set of practices. The other Christian practices are the means of contextual virtue for the preacher, as well as the directive content of preaching. The preaching life is embedded within a Christian life, a Christian life funds a rich preaching life, and a rich preaching life points the church to a comprehensively Christian life. This is the cycle of Christian formation from the perspective of the preacher.

The concepts of promise, presence, and command as outlined above also find the most satisfying unity once the person of God is understood to constitute their inherent unity. Just as the Spirit of Christ is the grace of God, which Christians wait upon in formative Christian practices, the presence of that Spirit as both promise and command comes to us as a call: "Follow me" (Matt 16:24). This call of discipleship gives with it both the indicative promise of presence and the command to choose "the better part" of life's potential practices (Luke 10:42). When the command of God is

---

42. Abraham and Kirby have suggested social holiness and social concern in *The Oxford Handbook of Methodist Studies*, 34. This language can be confusing given the difference between eighteenth-century meanings of the word social and current denotations and connotations. More significantly, these labels focus on the ends not the means. This section is seeking to outline the means.

understood to be at one with the promise of God's gracious presence, then practices of devotion and practices of compassion are not burdensome duties as some would fear. They do, though, remain acts of obedience.

Karl Barth has described the choice of obedience or disobedience to the call of Christ in this way, "If we will not bear the yoke of Jesus, we have to bear the yoke we ourselves have chosen, and it is a hundred times more heavy."[43] It is a burden not of duty but of obedience that relieves the burden of our own attempts to invent happiness.

If these practices are understood as piecemeal possibilities for the Christian, suggested helps for the Christian to add to his life, they become burdensome. When the pursuit of these practices is a way of life, not an addition to a way of life, they are an excellent freedom.[44] They root the Christian way of life in the pursuit of God who is our fulfillment and happiness. A life of practicing faith is central to practicing the preaching life. The means of grace provide the graces (virtues) for preaching to accomplish its functions and achieve its aims more easily and more joyfully.

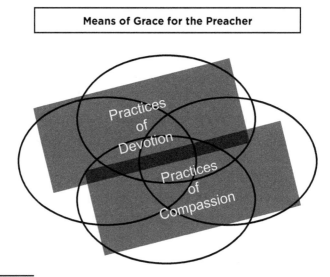

Means of Grace for the Preacher

Practices of Devotion

Practices of Compassion

---

43. Karl Barth, Geoffrey William Bromiley, and Kenneth C. Hanson, *The Call to Discipleship* (Minneapolis: Fortress Press, 2003), 31.

44. See Serene Jones, "Graced Practices: Excellence and Freedom in the Christian Life," in Volf and Bass, *Practicing Theology*, 42–75. Jones bases excellent freedom on justification (freedom) and sanctification (excellence). Though potentially theologically troubling if separated, the concept is compelling.

I learned to backpack as a teenager with a scouting troop in the Appalachian Mountains. We were taught to "be prepared," which many of us took to mean be prepared to stay comfortable in any kind of circumstance. This meant extra clothes, extra food, and lots of extra weight. Our scoutmaster who felt it was also his job to be prepared for all the boys who might not be prepared, carried an eighty-pound pack. The weight in our packs required metal support in the backpacks leading to heavier backpacks. Our boots were heavier in order to prevent ankles rolling from the weight of the packs. A twelve-mile day was an accomplishment.

My backpacking adventures took me up and down the Appalachian Trail, North Country Trail, Lake Superior Trail, Sheltowee Trace Trail, Colorado Trail, and other paths. Always there were blisters, rolled ankles, sore backs, and shorter-mile days. A mentor of mine, Keith Drury, talked to me about backpacking and made radical suggestions.

His philosophy was gleaned from the ultra-light guru Ray Jardine. Cut the pack weight by buying a smaller backpack. Then you are limited in what you can pack by the bag itself and the bag weighs less. Food is just fuel for the body, nothing more. So, eliminate the cooking gear using uncooked food. Bring just enough clothes. You can wash along the way. Ditch the boots and wear tennis shoes lightening your feet by over a pound each. Carry an ultra-light tent using a walking stick for a pole. Following these and other instructions my pack weight reduced from forty-five pounds to sixteen pounds not counting water. My next big hiking trip was 125 miles. Previously blisters typically formed within one day of hiking. A rolled ankle often occurred within the first fifty miles. This trip, I enjoyed 125 miles blister and injury free.

After hiking ten miles one morning we stopped for a break on top of a mountain pass in the Rockies. I was walking around instead of lying down. Keith looked at me and laughed. He said, "You know it is a light pack when you forget to take it off and don't even need to sit down." The backpacking culture I was a part of had me so convinced I needed to bring more in my backpack in order to be comfortable. The truth was, the less I worried about comfort, the more comfortable I became. Previously I had too big a backpack allowing me to carry too many extras to be comfortable.

Many preachers need a smaller backpack for their lives. We have bought the lies of consumerism, technological advances, and capitalistic cultures: stuff makes us happy, more stuff makes us more happy. We are so worried about our comfort we have become overburdened, uncomfortable, and unhappy. Our abundance requires maintenance. The time we spend on our technological escapes prevents time for contemplation, reflection, journaling, and prayer. Good food is one of our greatest comforts. How could we fast? Our lives are busy chasing happiness, how could we have more time to spend with the poor?

In spiritual formation courses for pastors many find they only engage in a few Christian practices in any regular way. Those they practice are not pursued with a confident trust in the presence and grace of God. Often the practices are a legalistic burden of duty. When the whole picture of the Christian life is presented, at first it seems too burdensome to imagine. In class, as we examine the portions of students' lives that are optional, added, even overly indulged, more and more space opens for the Christian life.

Consistently by the end, the Christian life is more restful, more meaningful, more inspiring, and liberating for the preachers than the mixed life they had been living. Universally the preachers feel they have much, much more to say. This last realization must be underscored for the purpose of the preaching life. Any flattening, diluting, or eliminating of a Christian way of life flattens, dilutes, and limits the available sources for preaching.

If practicing the Christian life seems like it would be too big of a burden it is probably because we cannot imagine adding it to the lifestyle "backpack" we are already carrying. We need to change lifestyles first (backpacks) and only carry what Christ's life will bear.

Scripture then remains so very important to practicing preachers, but not nearly as important as following the Spirit in a loving way of life. Within these practices we are humbled and lifted up at the same time. We gain empathy and compassion we could not gain some other way. We participate in the life of God and have much more to say about it than any sermon series could contain. We gain the courage to do justice from the faces and stories we encounter. And in all of this the willingness to obey the call of Christ to "follow" him into a life of love opens the opportunity to receive the promise "I will be with you always."

For Reflection

1. Turn to appendix D. In the margin next to each practice, score it according to the following rubric based on how you engage the practice:

   4 = regularly and joyfully
   3 = occasionally and meaningfully
   2 = once or twice a year
   1 = never

   As you do this, pray God would help you be honest but not self-shaming. What does this reveal to you about the shape of your life? How could you begin to switch lifestyles (change backpacks), not merely add more things to do?

2. Are there any zones of Christian practices you are more faithful to than others? Why might some categories of Christian practice be stronger than others for you? For those to whom you minister?

3. This chapter claims *contextual virtues* (centered humility, compassionate empathy, participatory wisdom, and courageous justice) are formed by the grace of God in these practices. Take time to try and discern which practices seem to best form which virtues.

4. The twin or polarizing dangers of *legalism* (a strict, literal conformity to religious law and obligations) and *antinomianism* (the belief that grace does not require moral obedience, and that moral obedience blocks the fulfillment of God's purposes for us) could be placed at either end of a spectrum. Which side of the spectrum do you tend to fall toward? Which side does your community fall toward? Some communities are

legalistic about one category of practices and antinomian about another. Is this true for you or a community you are a part of?

5. Take some time to journal about how you discern the Spirit is leading you in becoming a practicing Christian. Consider any of the following prompts: What first steps of personal change can you discern? How might "keeping in step with the spirit" keep this from becoming one more memory of anxious striving? What defenses do you have? How can God help you overcome them?

6. Take some time to consider how a more complete view of Christian practices can diversify the content for your preaching. How might a recent sermon have changed? What further means of receiving God's grace might be added to a coming sermon as a result of a more comprehensive view of the Christian life?

7. Study appendix C to better understand how the practices form the virtues, the virtues sustain the functions, and the functions enable the aim of preaching. How does this change the way you think about helping someone learn to preach? How might it change your own perspective on what it means to "prepare" a sermon?

CHAPTER 6
Rhythms for Preaching Practice

On the last day of our final preaching course the professor gave us a calm but impassioned speech. "This is the last thing I want you to hear me say: preach the Word." He handed out cards with the verse, "Preach the word...in season and out of season (2 Tim 4:2)," printed on the front. It was a moving moment hearing our old professor share what he felt were the most important words he could give us. He hoped for a pulpit rich with content, backed by hours of study, and the fruit of faithful wrestling with scriptures to find the Word of God through them. He hoped for deep and life-forming proclamation free of pandering attempts at relevance. What it means to preach the Word has been complicated and deepened for me over the years. The card is lost. Yet I still see that card in my mind often as I prepare once again to preach.

At the heart of preaching is interpretation, meaning making, or hermeneutics.[1] Preaching is a meaning-making life. The Christian canon is the focal point of Christian tradition and Christian worship. Preachers know the scriptures are both the great treasure and the great trouble of the church. The treasure is found in the reliability of the Spirit to give scriptures new voice in each succeeding generation of Christian preaching. This happens in spite of gaps between the worlds of the authors, the internal world of the text, and the worlds listeners live in now. Like any text, it requires interpretation. The trouble with Scriptures is a history

---

1. Hermeneutics is the art and science of interpreting texts.

of misinterpretation of these scriptures laced with racism, colonialism, sexism, greed, and atrocious violence.

The treasure of Scriptures leads many to adopt what has been labeled a *hermeneutic of tradition*. A hermeneutic of tradition envisions the job of the preacher as a steward; a caretaker of the great good handed down in the faith. In one version of the hermeneutic of tradition the preacher recognizes the world of thought, meaning, culture, and time in which she lives. She brings that world consciously to the task of reading scripture, seeking to discern the world of the text. The world is made up of the perceptions, culture, beliefs, and experiences she carries with her to the text. The world of the text is made up of differing perceptions, cultures, beliefs, contexts, and time. In this way the interpreter is not standing across time from an author. The world of the preacher is confronted by the world of the scriptural author. Those two worlds meet at their horizons in a collision that causes friction, conviction, resistance, and many other experiences until finally the horizons find some way to fuse. Some part of the world of the text has transformed some part of the world of the reader. Some part of the reader's world has added meaning to the world of the text.

The trouble with the Scriptures leads many to adopt what has been labeled a *hermeneutic of suspicion*. Because the world of the interpreter has often overpowered the world of the text, and because the world of the text often has within it sinful and abusive actions, the preacher has to come to the text with a certain suspicious gaze. The interpretations of tradition cannot always be trusted. Think of the collusion of the Christian world with the institution of slavery for one now-accepted, once-embattled example. The interpreter's first task, in a hermeneutic of suspicion, is to peel back the layers of meaning, translation, and corrupted interpretation to try and arrive at a meaning that brings life and justice to the world. Often this takes the form of differing emphases or presumptions about the text. Some texts the tradition has taken as "prescriptive" (do this) are recognized to be "descriptive" (this is). Rather than perpetuating the Fall as if the cursed nature of humanity were God's desire (do this), the preacher proclaims God's desire to redeem the Fall we are all affected by (this is). Narratives are not taken to be normative but are often read through the lens of a scriptural norm not held within a particular story.

There is a way for these two hermeneutics to strengthen rather than alienate each other. Though the language of tradition and suspicion is much newer language for hermeneutics and for preaching, the ancient church struggled with this tension as well. The rule of faith (*regula fidei*) and the law of love (*lex dilectionis*) marked some of the earliest church writings as a description of this struggle in the form of a solution. The rule of faith was the inherited tradition of the apostolic witness of scriptures, creeds, the early church theologians, and eventually the great councils of the church. This "rule" provided a boundary within which the interpreter could play. The law of love overruled any interpretation violating the second portion of the great commandment (love thy neighbor), even if that interpretation was the traditional one. In this way, Christian interpreters were able to hold the tradition in one hand, and suspicion in the form of love for neighbor in the other. Unfortunately, the history of the church shows the rule of faith growing ever more cumbersome with increasing traditions, and the rule of love becoming primarily defined by the tradition, with decreasing authority to rupture tradition.

These two poles, tradition/faith and suspicion/love, form the tension that pulls on the heart and mind of the preacher each time a sermon is being born. Though there are methodical ways of engaging this practice of interpretation, preachers do better to recognize the organic and somewhat unpredictable nature of interpretation. Following a method of interpretation for preaching is good and helpful, but do not be surprised when the real meaning making happens outside of the method in the entertaining of God's messengers unawares. An interpretive method only prepares us to discover meaning; it does not always deliver it.

A hermeneutic of tradition, something like a rule of faith, helps the preacher avoid suffering the mistakes of the early church again and again. The tradition of the doctrines surrounding creation, incarnation, redemption, resurrection, judgment, and life everlasting provides a plentiful playing field for the preacher. The dual nature of Christ as defined at Chalcedon is a textured guide for preaching. The aseity of God, God's lack of any external source for existence or need, is often a rich resource for preaching to humans who are to some degree the opposite. The simplicity of the Trinity—God is not composed of parts—could fill an entire sermon series. We do not always have to come up with "something to say," for something has already been spoken for us to hear in new ways. This does not mean there are not new insights to be had. A well-trained preacher can bring both old and new insights out of the scriptures and the doctrines that emerged from it. The Christian tradition has the ability to hand to us a rich playbook for preaching. It is a playbook that has loved mercy and done justice in innumerable ways before us and will long after we are gone. Yet, for many who read this paragraph who have experience with tradition's dark side, warning bells will go off. These bells remind us that tradition has at times abused, persecuted, and killed.

A hermeneutic of suspicion helps the preacher stand back and examine her own assumption of the meaning or implication of the tradition she has received. Often this meaning is troubled, questioned, and deepened through the preaching process. This "traditioning" includes within it adjusting, clarifying, even opposing old interpretations. The natural question for most preachers is how to guide a hermeneutic of suspicion. It scares the preacher who wants to believe there is only one interpretation of scripture, and that interpretation should be clear and obvious to any reader of the text. The unfortunate reality is our prejudices, experiences, communities of interpretation, preaching memories, and more can cloud our ability to see and hear much of what the text says and means. This is why it is so important to practice the preaching life, not only to write sermons.

The preaching life is not limited to interpreting the text, discerning meaning, crafting a sermon, and delivering that sermon. The preaching life weaves itself among the movements of the Christian life. The practices of devotion root the preacher in the rule of faith. These practices continually plant resources of Christian faith within the preacher so that the preacher never writes a sermon from a blank page, never interprets as a lone voice. The more immersed a preacher is in ongoing prayer, searching the scriptures, communal worship, communion, baptism services, fasting, Sabbath rest, and listening to the Word proclaimed, the more that preacher has to offer in each and every sermon.

The preaching life is not only funded by practices of devotion, however. Practices of justice and compassion rupture the world of the cloistered preacher calling her out into the world, suffering and rejoicing with others. It is through these practices of reconciliation, incarnate care, opposing injustice, or undoing oppression that the preacher discovers what portions of his traditional interpretations are invalidated by the rule of love. The preacher does not have to muster up a hermeneutic of suspicion when those who suffer from unjust uses of scripture are in his life in regular and meaningful ways. The hermeneutic of suspicion often comes through friendship as a gift. Then the new lens for interpreting scripture helps practices of devotion become practices filled with compassion; the rule of faith moves closer to the law of love.

In my own preaching life, though reading has helped me immensely, a hermeneutic of suspicion has come to me more specifically through relational encounters than study of books. A friend in ministry helped me see the jar the woman at the well left behind was parallel to the nets for the disciples. A neighbor whose last name still bears the marks of slavery helped me see that Joseph enslaved many nations. A friend in the Philippines helped me realize scripture never condemns the giving of bribes; in corrupt governments certain bribes may be required for the poor to survive. It does condemn those who require bribes—the powerful who use their power to exploit the poor. A colleague shared at coffee recently the verse from Deuteronomy, "But there will be no poor among you . . . if only you will strictly obey the voice of the LORD your God" (15:4-5, ESV), as a rupturing verse for the wealthy's favored verse, "The poor will always be with you" (John 12:8, ESV). James 1:27 moves beyond orphans and widows when a friend mentioned these were simply ancient society's forgotten and vulnerable ones. Ours might also include single mothers, foster children graduated from the system with only dysfunctional families in their lives, or others. A friend and spiritual director who is single wakened me more deeply to the privileged place traditional marriage is given in the church's interpretations of passages, even texts that give priority to singleness.

Preachers in my courses go to nursing homes, homeless missions, immigration centers, prisons, food banks, and mentoring programs for foster children. In our debriefing and reflection discussions it is clear the experiences teach on their own if preachers simply come in attempting to be contextually virtuous. One student was troubled by the phrase *homeless person* or *homeless people* for its implications of shamed identity. The group suggested most of us could think of ourselves as "people who are currently middle class," recognizing our frailty and possibility of becoming "homeless people." In the same discussion session other students addressed societal evaluations of the elderly as "useless," mistreatment of minority religious groups, and the tendency to ignore scriptures that speak about justice while elevating scriptures that speak about wholeheartedness, devotion, or holiness.

A hermeneutic of tradition and a hermeneutic of suspicion are united in and through the Christian practices of devotion and compassion as means of grace. The practices form the interpretive backdrop for the study of scripture for the pastor. A pastor who is not practicing the Christian life will find it more burdensome than necessary to practice the preaching life. The reverse is the fear of the busy pastor. If I engage those practices, how will I craft a sermon for Sunday? How will I still have time to lead? Will my family suffer? When practicing the preaching life as an extension of Christian life a sermon helps to write itself in the most unexpected of ways. The rest of life also becomes more beautiful, fulfilling, and unified.

If the above is true, preparing to preach is no longer fully separated from pastoral care, ministry with the poor, or personal pursuit of God. The impulse to divide Christian practices from Christian preaching comes from a desire to make sure the pastor receives from God for herself, not only for others. The nurturing of the soul of the preacher is the aim. The challenge is many preachers enact this divide between discovering sermons and worshipping God. Then they gradually experience a demoralizing disconnection between their spiritual lives and their preaching lives. The goal should be abundance of insights from scripture, too many to preach. When abundance of life-shifting wisdom from scripture arrives through both personal and pastoral exegesis, worry over spiritual dryness disappears. The division between pastoral and personal remains, but is porous.[2]

Instead of dividing any sentiments of devotion from disciplined sermon study, preachers need to practice *delaying*. It is very tempting to treat sermon making like stir-frying. Preaching is much more of a slow cooker meal. When the insights a preacher finds (through the Christian life or the preaching life) are allowed to settle into the heart of the preacher, then the insights mature, deepen, and intermingle. The flavors of the meal have time to integrate, the tenderness of the meal is easier to consume, and the aroma begins to surround the preacher in compelling ways. If the delay between insight and preaching is too short, humility, empathy, wisdom, and justice have not had time to shift the preacher's perspective. Remind the preacher of others' suffering. Engage the preacher in a personal struggle. Unmask the preacher's hidden defenses. Open the preacher's eyes to evil in structures and systems. If we do not significantly delay the *use* of discovered personal meaning, most preachers will end up making their preaching an extension of their own personal issues rather than a service to the church. Lengthening the time between discovery and delivery overcomes the fear of "professional Christians" much better than removing a spirit of worship from sermonic preparation.

This is true partially because preachers do not merely interpret passages of scripture. Preachers interpret life, which takes time. This happens by using scripture as a lens for life, and life as a lens for scripture. This circle between life and interpretation can be understood as a cycle or spiral of interpretation. (1) The hermeneutical spiral starts with a preconceived interpretation of a text. All preachers start with presumed

---

2. This is not to suggest that pastoral and personal identity be mixed or confused. The ability to de-role and have an identity separate from professional accomplishment or role is of course very crucial to ministerial well-being. Distinction is necessary. Pastors must be able to distinguish between their professional identity (added on, "pastor") and their personal identity (integral to, "child of God").

meanings. (2) The preacher engages critical study (through both tradition and suspicion). This often includes syntactical study, translation, word studies, literary analysis, historical background, lexicons, theological dictionaries, and critical commentaries. Preachers do not use all of these tools each time, but master preachers use many of them each time.[3] (3) The preacher experiences a necessary disorientation. The critical study alienates the text from the preacher, forcing her to recognize the foreignness of the text and its unexpected voice. At times this disorientation comes not from the text itself, but from another's contrasting interpretation. Othering the text releases the text from captivity to our presumptions. (4) This disorientation forces time for reflection and discussion with others. Journaling, contemplative prayer, discussion with preaching partners, and mental processing all serve to reintegrate the disorienting data. (5) The preacher discovers new meaning in the text and in life. The text projects new possibilities into the life of the preacher, and the life of the preacher brings out new implications from the text. (6) The preacher then reintegrates the new meaning of the text into forms and practices of life. In it all, the spiral is a double helix formed by the rule of faith (tradition) and the law of love (suspicion).

A Four-Week Rhythm for Preaching Preparation

A cursory consideration of all that is involved in this interpretive cycle should lead the preacher to realize this takes time, space, skillful interpretation, personal energy, and help. For this reason, most preachers are not helped by starting Monday to study for a sermon Sunday. If the preaching life is practiced on a six-day cycle, the delay between insight and proclamation is too short. The voices of others have not had enough time to

---

3. The tools of biblical exegesis, if pursued for every sermon the way they are often taught, would become too burdensome for any preacher. It would be like a master carpenter emptying the van of all its tools and resources into each home at every job. A trustworthy artisan knows the best tools for the particular time and place. A lazy worker skips the best method and tools in order to cut corners and save time. It is central to any craft to learn the difference.

rupture the presumed meaning. The strangeness of the text has not had a chance to disorient the preacher fully. The pressure to have something to preach burdens the preaching life and creates great stress on the preacher. Most preachers need a new method for sermon study in order to live in peace. It needs to be a method that places preaching preparation regularly on the calendar with plenty of time to prepare, pray, reflect, engage the Christian life, and discover a sermon along the way.

The challenge of offering methods for sermon study is that every preacher has a personality, unique patterns of life, differing work rhythms/ expectations, and differing roles. Here are some common critiques of preaching methods pastors often offer for preaching books in classes or conferences: "This does not seem to fit bi-vocational pastors." "Why are preaching methods always so local-church focused?" "I do not have a library nearby." "This seems like it is for senior pastors. I only preach once a month." "What changes if I am preaching to (insert a context, age, or culture)?" The method presented in this section will be more flexible than most Monday-to-Sunday sermon study methods. However, no book written for a general audience will fit all particular preachers. I think of friends in the Philippines, South Korea, Haiti, Liberia, Ghana, Latin America, and other contexts knowing there is no one-size-fits-all preaching method. Bi-vocational pastors in any culture have widely varying structures to their weeks. Each context will have to particularize from the following schedule and method what is necessary for their culture and setting. At the same time, in each of these contexts one common realization emerges when interviewing preachers: time is the primary concern and the most significant obstacle to overcome.

Review the table below briefly to familiarize yourself with the overall concept. Then read through the day by day description to get a better feel for the meaning of the table, and how it would work in a ministry week. The reflection section at the end of the chapter will guide you through crafting your own preaching-preparation process fitted to your own ministry rhythms.

TABLE 1

Four Weeks of Preaching, with Fridays Off

	M	T	W	TR	F	Sat	Sun
Past Sermon	-	CF	-	-	-	-	-
Sermon I	IOW/PR1	OW	@	PR1	-	PR2	■
Sermon II	R&Q/Ob	Ob/L	PG/E	IOW	-	-	
Sermon III	R	-	-	-	-	-	-
Sermon IV	-	-	-	-	-	R	-

Key:

CF	constructive feedback session
IOW	improvisational expression, outlining, writing
OW	outline and write after having spoken through major sections of the sermon
PR1	try to preach through a majority of the sermon in a start and stop fashion
@	submit material to worship leaders
PR2	preach from A to Z without stops, in order to polish and/or shorten the sermon (timed)
PR3	preach the sermon again from A to Z if time allows
L	translate or other original language work (word study, parsing, etc.)
Ob	make detailed observations for 15+ minutes
PG	preaching group discussion
E	exegetical reading (critical commentaries and other supporting sources)
R	a simple unhurried reading of the text in the preacher's native language
R&Q	a slow re-reading accompanied by notation of a few beginning questions
Shaded box	the preaching day (sermon I)

1. The day after preaching

Though many full-time preachers take a day off on Monday,[4] I have been convinced by ministers who think it usually better to take a Sabbath rest on Friday. Delaying your sermon process by taking a day off undoes the momentum from the previous day and reduces the time between discovery and delivery. If the day off is Friday, and Sunday's sermon is 95 percent finished, the mind can rest as well as the body.[5] On Monday, or the day after preaching, consider scheduling at least two hours to read and study. First, read the text for nearly three weeks from now (sermon III). Read it in a relaxed way simply soaking in what comes to mind. The goal is to be a little more familiar with the passage. It does not need to take more than ten minutes. Then open the passage for next week (sermon II), thirteen days away. For this passage take the time to mark notes, underline, and ask questions to guide your interpretive work. This should not take more than twenty to thirty minutes.

One technique many preachers find helpful at this beginning stage is three-column interpretation. In the first column write the heading "detailed observations." These notes can be as simple as "The passage begins with the word *because*." Then, in the second column, note questions. For example, "Why does the author need to support his claim with what follows? What are the specific supports the author uses? What are their significance for this passage?" The third column contains beginning interpretations or hunches. For example, "The passage assumes the reader needs more than just a statement of what is true. We need reasons to believe it is true. In other words, Paul assumes we will doubt. Paul assumes we will wrestle. Paul assumes our faith needs reason."

Doing this for a passage thirteen days away gives the mind plenty of time to process the material details of the passage. When words or

---

4. If you regularly preach on Wednesday, or some other day, simply think of Monday as "the day after preaching." Then Monday could be a helpful Sabbath. The challenge is, you do not get the weekend effect when nothing is scheduled for Saturday.

5. Staff pastors do not always get to choose their day off. I also recognize youth ministry's need for Friday work is nearly universal. See table 2 in pages that follow for a chart-based version of this section for Mondays off. Appendix E contains a day-by-day summary in paragraph form. Personalize it to fit your ministry needs. Pastors in coaching and conferences consistently name these charts as central to efforts to revitalize their preaching.

concepts are not understood, writing down the question helps keep the preacher faithful to the necessary study to understand them. With practice, even fifteen to thirty minutes of three-column interpretation can produce significant amounts of meaning. Having these beginning meanings in hand almost ensures the sermon for two weeks in advance will begin to "write itself" in the midst of the flow of life.[6]

The rest of the time can be spent on this week's sermon (sermon I). Open the passage for this coming Sunday you studied last week. Review your exegetical notes, spend time in contemplative prayer, and seek to move the sermon forward. For external processors this usually means improvisational preaching then outlining and writing. For internal processors, this often means reflection, outlining, then improvisational preaching (out loud) or free writing. The aim is to craft the sermon in a way that flows *for the ear* not the eye. The sooner the sermon becomes "heard" the sooner it will flow and relieve the preacher's anxiety. For many preachers a car, an empty house, or a lonely place in nature provides space to test the sermon out loud. External processors will often start in these spaces, and then later outline and write. Return to exegetical resources briefly in any place where uncertainties remain.

2. *Two days after preaching*

Many ministers, particularly in multi-staff congregations, have in-house meetings on Tuesdays. This may not be the case for your situation. If it is, two days after preaching is a perfect time to receive the feedback you were not ready to receive the day of, or the day after. You may have feedback forms you saved from Sunday or texts, messages, or e-mails, or you may schedule conversations with a small group or team. Communal feedback helps build the humility and empathy a preacher needs to have in order to gain wisdom and justice. Inevitably we have blind spots and need the corrective care a loving team can provide.

---

6. When guiding preachers personally, I suggest preachers only begin three-column interpretation or detailed observations on the day after preaching (for a sermon twelve or thirteen days away). If only a few questions are noted, it is enough. Pressure to do more may cause procrastination. Freedom to do less may trick the preacher into wanting to do more.

The feedback session can best serve the preacher when it starts with descriptive affirmations that are concrete, specific, and genuine. This should not be diminished or seen as a "padding" for the real "critique." What is good is what should be grown and multiplied and is likely therefore the most helpful feedback a preacher receives. The more specific and concrete the affirmations are, the more the preacher is able to repeat them in the future. Then the team should offer constructive suggestions, not critiques. Do not tell the preacher what to avoid. Do share with the preacher suggestions to make the preaching in the future better than it already was. Finally, the team should offer words of encouragement related to the preacher's ministry as a whole, not the sermon moment alone. A discerning community continues to name what they believe God is doing through the preacher and will continue to do. These feedback sessions are not merely a "best practice." If done well, these are communal ways of reflecting what meaning was made, what meaning was misunderstood, and what meaning was lost in the preaching moment.[7]

For this week's coming sermon (sermon I), Tuesday is usually a good day to polish the detailed outline or manuscript to the point of discernible sermon form.[8] If all has gone well, this is not a large leap for the sermon to make. This may require free writing or more verbal preaching attempts to help the sermon cohere. The sermon should not be forced into a form but allowed to emerge organically. Then once it is well on its way, a sermon form that best fits the sermon can be discerned. This way the sermon form helps fill in the gaps instead of restrict the sermon to a mold.

Metaphors can be forced, even should be. This is the day when preachers can "play" with the meaning they have found by forcing it to be illustrated by anything that comes to mind or accosts the eye. A sweater becomes an illustration of grace, a remote an illustration of the invisible activity of God, a family photo an illustration of inauthenticity, a marker an illustration of sin, or opening the curtain becomes an illustration of discernment. The preacher holds each of these potential metaphors against the findings of exegesis with a critical eye. Then, once the metaphor is run back through the grid of interpretation, she chooses

---

7. More often than not, a silent but note-taking posture is best for the preacher in these sessions. Defending or deflecting will only reduce honest feedback in the future. You do not have to agree.

8. Chapter 9 explores living sermon forms for practicing the preaching life.

the most fitting metaphors and images for the focus and function of the sermon. If pastoral meetings come early in the day, feedback helps guide the outline. If pastoral meetings come late in the day, outlining provides an opportunity to discuss communally what the preacher is planning.

If the schedule allows, next week's text can be examined more closely now that this week's sermon is far enough along. It is difficult to discipline the preacher to set the sermon aside for this week, but it is crucial for the sermon to marinate in the subconscious. Next week's text can be translated if the preacher has the skills. If the preacher cannot translate, the text can be examined in an interlinear method to discern what is underneath the hood of the translations being used. At the very least, the typical "word studies" or lexicon study is needed to make observations based on the original language's tone and connotations.[9] Often the setting aside of this week's sermon and picking up of next week's sermon is all it takes for surprise moments of creative insight to emerge, as though from an unexpected corner.

In terms of time requirements, many preachers find no extra time is needed from their schedule for the constructive feedback as meetings are already scheduled. The outlining of this week's sermon and the textual work for next week can often be fit into an hour or an hour and a half of focused attention. This is dependent on previous sermonic work.

3. *Three days after preaching*

Wednesday is often the day by which a worship pastor, song leader, music director, or worship arts team hopes to have the sermon's outline, slides, or other media. This gives other members of the team time to best do their job particularly if the worship team has practices on Wednesday nights. Whether or not the preacher has the luxury of this kind of team, it also gives the preacher a deadline. Deadlines help force the preacher to stop agonizing over the possibilities and commit to at least a general direction, form, and desired response. The Wednesday goal for this week's

---

9. For the average pastor without translation capacity, sufficient recourses for original language work are now available freely online on websites that offer interlinear versions, concordances, lexicons, word usage, and more. Developing world or rural pastors without libraries will find these resources even more invaluable.

sermon is a submitted set of these materials to anyone helping the entire service come together as a whole.

When weeks go as planned, the week's core sermon outline and supporting materials are settled by Wednesday. Changes may be made later, but the primary structure is clear. Next week's text has been read, observed, and studied according to the original language. It is best to write a best-guess summary of what the text is trying to say and do prior to reading exegetical commentaries and historical background materials. This forces the preacher to name her hunches and stay honest with her misconceptions. Naming this guess only takes a few minutes. Then an hour can be given to reading commentaries, researching historical background material, and researching other scholarly material by diverse authors.[10] Though it is sometimes difficult to find commentaries by diverse authors, multiple perspectives are crucial to hearing the text well. This studious reading helps the preacher discern the passage's background, missed details, and puzzling ambiguities. At the end of this time, a spoken and rewritten claim for next week's passage will help the preacher integrate the reading and bring it closer to sermonic unity.

Many preachers practice communal forms of study and sermon preparation. The regular face-to-face meeting with laypeople and ministers who are studying the same text can help preaching's richness immensely. It is impossible to predict when the best time for these meetings will be for diverse preachers. Some are scheduled and structured weekly gatherings. Others are once-a-month support groups. Many preachers simply have a few go-to people they turn to when preparing a sermon via email or phone. Though this method calls for the preacher to engage community on Wednesday, eleven days out from the sermon, the preacher will have to experiment to find the best sequence.

4. Four days after preaching

Thursday is a day when many loose ends need to be tied up if Friday is to be a day off. The only schedulable task is to begin outlining or free writing next week's sermon. As one senior pastor in North Carolina

---

10. Some will think this mark of an hour to be insufficient. At times this is true. The preacher has to learn when more is required and when less is more. I have listened to many sermons that would have been helped by less commentary reading, and more insight into life itself. Of course, we have all experienced the thin sermon that was a victim of the reverse.

recently told me, "The sermon after I have a week off is always better than the rest." The reason may simply be that the particular sermon had more time to marinate. Even a half hour of reflection on the next sermon will yield incredible momentum for the next week (sermon II). The primary task of the day is to find half an hour in between other duties to try and preach the sermon for this week (sermon I) from beginning to end.[11] Most preachers are helped by minimal use of notes, allowing the sermon to emerge as they can remember it out loud. This way the sermon moves by logic of verbal association (one thing naturally reminds you of the next) rather than forced form. Rehearsal often takes no additional time from the minister's day. Commuting to the hospital, nursing home, and prison or even running errands all provide significant time in the car to birth the sermon aloud. If the preacher lives in contexts where car rides are rare, long walks can take their place. The worst-case scenario on a busy week requires the preacher to sneak out of the house for thirty minutes in the evening to find a lonely place to preach.

5. Five days after preaching

Friday is the golden day, the minister's "Sabbath" in terms of rest from work. The sermon from this week may not be polished, but it is ready enough. Next week's sermon is already in rough outline form. The mind can relax. The body can rest. All that is suggested for this day is to do whatever restores mind, body, and spirit. Restful reading for pleasure, hands-on hobbies that are not too demanding, contemplative prayer, and journaling are all good medicine for the preacher's quieted self. The bi-vocational pastor will have to swap Friday for some other day, usually Saturday. If this is the case, rigid discipline to make sure the sermon is completely polished is crucial for the minister's long-term well-being. It is worth a half hour here or there to practice preaching the message on Friday so that Saturday can be a day of rest.

---

11. This is based on congregational expectations of preaching styles, often expecting less than thirty-minute sermons. Fifteen-minute sermons may take less time, though some amount of false starts and unexpected stops adds time. A thirty-minute sermon expectation may still only require thirty minutes on this day. Often the "extra" comes through the addition of an introduction and more targeted conclusion that were not clear the week before.

6. Six days after preaching

Saturday may hold prayer breakfasts, fund-raisers, special events, weddings, or other culturally determined ministry activities. These are hard to predict, and the preaching requirements for the day must flex to the unpredictability. Some days, Saturdays can be mostly time for family and friendship connections. Other Saturdays require more. For multiple service congregations, Saturday may not be very free. Because of the variable nature of the day, all this method suggests for passage study is a prayerful reading of the passage for three weeks from now (sermon IV). Do not take notes, write down questions, or mark the passage except for the enrichment of your soul. At some point in the day, find space to preach the coming sermon's major movements aloud until they can flow smoothly from beginning to end. Consider timing the sermon so that you are able to shorten it as necessary. Since thirty minutes may be enough, treasure any moments to drive, take a walk, or be in your home or office alone and undisturbed. The only goal is to make sure each movement of the sermon is internalized as its own unit and flows together well with the whole.

7. Preaching day

Every seven days the day comes again for the weekly preacher. Many preachers find it helpful to rise early this day and in the quiet morning hours rehearse the sermon from beginning to end. This makes all the transitions come to mind, solidifies the beginning and ending, and gives the preacher confidence the sermon will unfold naturally. Most preachers benefit from either a verbal or a written manuscript. External processors often eschew written manuscripts yet craft the sermon out loud and rehearse it enough for each word to have its own place. Manuscript or no, rewriting the sermon into a basic outline reminds the preacher of moves and transitions so that the sermon becomes a map in the mind. Manuscripts for the actual sermon moment can be very helpful, but only if the preacher is free enough from the manuscript to be able to engage the congregation, embody the sermon, and adjust the delivery in response to visual and verbal cues from the worshipping community.

This way of practicing the preaching life has helped preachers who have been willing to give it a try. Often the preachers I talk to remind me of the rich young ruler. They know they want something more joyful than what they have. They have worked hard to practice the fundamentals of preaching and to polish the skills. "All this I have done," they say to exegesis, writing sermon claims, focus and function statements, outlines, manuscripts, and sermon forms. When I suggest this radical reorientation of their lives to make the preaching life more integrated with all of life, they walk away sad. It sounds like too high a cost. In truth, it is *easier* than the typical Monday-to-Sunday drudgery. Preachers simply cannot imagine starting any earlier than they already do. The good news is all that is required is reading the text to get the process started. The following chart has helped those preachers who prefer a Monday off cycle to their weekly rhythm. As with the other, it is a starting point for reflection not a rule for all preachers.

TABLE 2

Four Weeks of Preaching, with Mondays Off

	M	**T**	**W**	**TR**	**F**	**Sat**	**Sun**
Past Sermon	-	CF	-	-	-	-	-
Sermon I	-	IOW/ PR1	OW	@	PR1	PR2	■
Sermon II	-	R&Q/ Ob	Ob/L	PG/E	IOW	-	-
Sermon III	-	-	-	-	-	-	R
Sermon IV	-	-	-	-	-	R	-

Key:

CF	constructive feedback session
IOW	improvisational expression, outlining, writing
OW	outline and write after having spoken through major sections of the sermon
PR1	try to preach through a majority of the sermon in a start and stop fashion
@	submit material to worship leaders
PR2	preach from A to Z without stops in order to polish and/or shorten the sermon (timed)
PR3	preach the sermon again from A to Z if time allows
L	translate or other original language work (word study, parsing, etc.)
Ob	make detailed observations for 15+ minutes
PG	preaching group discussion
E	exegetical reading (critical commentaries and other supporting sources)
R	a simple unhurried reading of the text in the preacher's native language
R&Q	a slow re-reading accompanied by notation of a few beginning questions
Shaded box	the preaching day (sermon I)

117

After preaching, some preachers request others withhold feedback for two days. This gives the emotional world of the preacher time to recover and the psychological resources to be renewed. Spend time in contemplative prayer and rest. Do not feel guilty if one leads naturally to the next. The preacher who naps on preaching days is wise. Next week's sermon will improve if on the day of preaching you simply reread the passage for the coming Sunday. This five-minute practice helps the preacher look forward rather than backward and already begin to undo any anxiety about next week. After all, this passage has been read, reread, and studied, and a sermon is already coming to the fore. Now that this day's sermon is done, the mind can more fully work on the next week's sermon even as the preacher sleeps.

By breaking up the practice of meaning making and sermon crafting into smaller and more manageable sections of time, the preacher takes advantage of several things. First, the power of Christian practices to become interpretive lenses for preaching is increased. The whole world and all of life seems to open up as an illustration when a sermon is in the preacher's pocket. Second, the temptation to use any and every little experience, story, or personal encounter for the sermon is diminished when sermons begin to take shape more than one week in advance.[12] Since more illustrative and metaphorical material presents itself, preachers have time to choose the best material. Third, the gaps in life can be more effectively used. Five to ten minutes to read a scripture passage is not difficult to find. Five hours to complete an entire exegesis process is. Ten-minute gaps for improvisational attempts to preach sermon snippets abound in most pastors' lives. The burden to write an entire sermon in one sitting, however, is intimidating enough for even disciplined pastors to find creative forms of procrastination.

For Reflection

1. Take some time to write out your sermon-preparation process in steps. Include textual study, exegetical work, critical commentaries, prayer, writing the focus and function, outlining,

---

12. It is not a desirable situation for people in a preacher's life to constantly fear being "used" as an illustration for the coming sermon.

free writing or speaking, communal discussion, rehearsal, collaboration with worship teams, or other steps you think are important.

2. Look back at the steps you outlined for the preaching process. Is anything missing? Are any of the steps so large they will naturally encourage procrastination? Some things are too big to begin, for example reading the appropriate sections of three commentaries. Break those items down into more manageable steps.

3. Assuming there are no surprises of ministry, what days would you like each of the steps to occur in order to accomplish a four-week rhythm for preaching preparation? Use the proposed method of this chapter as a model to modify for your own life structures and capacities. There are two summary versions of this chapter's preparation process included for you in appendix E. One is for Fridays off, the other for Monday's off.

4. Go back through the list of steps and discern two or three that you could shorten or cut if ministry surprises did occur. All preachers have times when they have to cut corners. It is best to decide which corners to cut beforehand.

5. Can you think of a time when you allowed yourself enough time to integrate your sermon's claims into your life before preaching? Can you think of a time when you wish you had been able to have that time? What difference did the space for integration make in your preaching?

6. If you are preaching regularly already, you may find it intimidating to shift toward a four-week pattern. In order to move closer to the aim, consider simply reading the passages for three and four weeks out during this week. Next week do the same (read three and four weeks out). Also, add a little advanced work for the sermon for two weeks out such as detailed questioning and some original language work. The following week do the above, and try to write a beginning claim for next week's sermon by the end of the week. In the fourth week, enact the four-week pattern you have modified to fit your schedule in complete form. Journal about the difference the increased time makes as you work through the process.

CHAPTER 7
Speaking Meaning to Being

The philosopher Martin Heidegger once called language "the House of Being."[1] It is not good to confuse Heidegger's Being with the Word of Christianity. Yet something rings true about the metaphor. Words have a power that moves beyond meaning. Words evoke and even create new realities, realities in which we dwell. The compiler of Proverbs seems to agree: "Death and life are in the power of the tongue" (Prov 18:21). Words have more than meaning. They have power. Often the power of the words we use is not discovered until long after the sound of voices dies away.

J. L. Austin proposed we change how we think about language and the use of words through a category called speech acts. Speech-acts theory recognizes the active side of words. Words do simply say things (locutionary speech). Words also enact things simply by being said (illocutionary speech). Words also cause certain effects (perlocutionary speech).[2] The philosophical labels for the terms are not nearly as important as the meaning behind them. It is a little over simplistic but useful to think of it in this shorthand way: words say things, words do things, and words cause things.

A few examples will be helpful. Consider the simple phrase *I do*. It first *says something* that could be stated differently to highlight the content, "I,

---

1. For an accessible English translation that includes the "Letter on Humanism" in which this famous quote is found see *Martin Heidegger: Pathmarks*, ed. William McNeil (Cambridge: Cambridge University Press, 1998), 239ff.

2. J. L. Austin, *How to Do Things with Words* (London: Oxford University Press, 1962).

the very one speaking, affirm that the previously shared promise is one I am making today. I *do* in fact promise that, and *I* am the one promising it." Second, it *does something* simply by the act of saying it. Stating it certifies the commitment to marriage and creates a bond of promise between the two people publicly saying "I do." They are now married and have enacted that marriage verbally in public. *You're fired, I promise*, and *consider it done* all have similar qualities. They do something by saying something. Third, *I do* causes certain things. It persuades a significant other to merge bank accounts, convinces the clergyperson to make a pronouncement, and inspires the gathered witnesses with the sanctity of the moment. Whether or not these effects are intended, they are in fact accomplished by the words.

Why does this matter for preaching? Both the metaphor that labels language a "house of being" and the analysis of language as doing something, not just saying something, help to explain elements of the power of speech in preaching. Even from a human standpoint, without awareness of the spiritual, preaching holds within it power to bring things into being through spoken word. It also holds the power to settle, disrupt, rupture, or even undo things that once were.

One of the most often missed implications of these insights is that preaching has power to bring things to being *for the preacher*. When the preacher utters words in conversation with preaching partners, to God in prayer, out loud in improvisational rehearsal, or from the pulpit, those words have the power to bring things to being *for the preacher*. The words of preaching can become so powerful, they become home. This has significant effect on how we think about the discovery of meaning, the experience of the Word, conversation with others, and the crafting of the sermon.

First, if speech says, does, and effects things then multiple layers of verbalized preparation become more important. The preacher who interprets Scripture well, then reads Scripture aloud well, enacts the speech act of the Scripture upon the preacher to a greater degree than a historical-critical method alone can accomplish. Scientific methods pull apart and analyze; performative methods pull together and enact. Both are helpful, but many preachers do not realize the power of speaking the passage aloud in multiple ways in order to discern its meaning and to speak that meaning into being. Try reading this phrase silently, *Be still, and know that I am God* (Ps 46:10 ESV). Now, think through what each word means in the context of the sentence. Imagine the tone with which it should be said. And speak it out loud to yourself now. Do you sense the difference? Performing scripture, embodying scripture, speaking it aloud with faithful embodiment enacts the power of the words upon the speaker.

A second homiletical insight emerging from speech-act theory is preachers may be more like bats than owls. Owls have extraordinary vision even in the dark of night. Bats, however, find their food through the use of sonar waves sent outward, ricocheting off the tiniest of bugs to the ear of the bat. Bats locate their food by sound. Preaching is an oral/aural art, yet we often seek to discern the meaning visually, then deliver it orally. Scriptures were crafted in oral cultures and primarily intended for the ear not the eye. The oral cultures at the time scriptures were written naturally would have thought of orality as necessary for *discovering* meaning not only for *delivering* meaning.[3]

Preachers who test out the sounds of words, the impact of words, the force of words, and the effect of words aloud are coming closer to the message as it was intended (an oral text to an oral culture) and the medium (the oral/aural art of preaching). The effect of words on a page is not the same as the effect of words in the ear. The great Dallas pastor Zan Holmes shares, "I have gladly found that the best way to write for the ear is to talk the words onto the paper. In this way the words are tested on my ear, and I write them when I am convinced that they sound right and can be effectively heard in the language of my congregation. . . . By the same token I clearly understand that the sermon manuscript is *not* the sermon. Instead, it is a *step on the way* to the sermon."[4]

---

3. In this way Romans 10:17, "faith comes from hearing" is a multilayered thought. See the lectures captured in Walter J. Ong, *The Presence of the Word: Some Prolegomena for Cultural and Religious History* (Binghamton, NY: Global Publications, 2000).

4. Cleophus J. LaRue, ed., *Power in the Pulpit: How America's Most Effective Black Preachers Prepare Their Sermons* (Louisville, KY: Westminster John Knox Press, 2002), 80.

Often sermons are located when we "sound them out." Preachers can sound out their sermons improvisationally in their offices, their cars, their quiet homes, empty meadows, lonely woods, or with a group of preaching partners, or a multitude of other ways. Trying out portions of the sermon this way helps the preacher enact the message upon herself, feel the force of the words, and discern if the words resonate with, question, stand against, or stand under the text for the day. Even preachers who are hearing impaired benefit from the "speaking" of the texts through signing as a form of embodiment requiring emphasis, expression, and visible interpretation of the text.

For most preachers, the sooner orality is injected into the preaching process the better. It is tempting for introverted, internally processing preachers in particular to try and arrange every portion of the sermon on paper before allowing any words to come into auditory space. This can be constricting. First and foremost, it prevents the full effect of the words from reaching the preacher until late in the process when the concrete of the sermon is already poured into its form. Second, since this effect is delayed, the preacher may not find the true heart of the sermon. You hear a sermon's heart beat more than you read it. Third, because the sermon is conceived and arranged visually, the flow of the written sermon may never work in the preacher's "ears." This makes internalizing the sermon seem difficult, freedom from notes nearly impossible, and rigid adherence to a manuscript or detailed outline necessary.

If the sermon can be written verbally along the way and *captured* visually it is merely preserved rather than created in writing. Then a new dynamic occurs. The medium (preaching) now matches the message (scriptures) and the form of delivery (sermon) in its oral formation and auditory format. Further, the wording, sequence, cadence, tone, and volume are discerned together rather than separately making the message more naturally congruent with its delivery.

A few preachers in every group feel suddenly released from silent embarrassment when I share the concept of speaking meaning to being. "I thought I was crazy for having to do this. But I never could seem to get a sermon to form well without talking out loud about it," one pastor in a doctor of ministry course confessed to me.[5] Another said, "I thought I was the only one preaching toward a sermon in the shower, the car, the empty office, or the church sanctuary early in the morning."

One preacher I occasionally help in sermon crafting is an internally processing introvert. She resisted this concept strongly and still struggles with writing a sermon out loud on her own. Usually she sends written sermonic ideas in an email when she feels "stuck." On the phone she summarizes her sermon out loud to me. Then I narrate back to her what I think she has written or said in the sermon. As she hears the sermon come back to her in the other person's voice, the sermon comes together and flows much more easily. The key for her, and perhaps other internal processors or visual learners, is not to wait too long after crafting written ideas to verbalize them. The "flow" may come too late to create momentum for the sermon.

The oral/aural nature of preaching preparation for the preacher makes early preparation all the more important. If a preacher can do the exegetical work early enough, all of the gaps of a minister's life can become more productive and reduce the perceived burden of preaching preparation. The practices of ministry can also become preaching preparation if handled carefully. Asking a shut-in, hospitalized person, prison mentee, nursing home resident, or even nonbelieving skeptic to share his perceptions of a coming passage can be empowering to him and, more important, rupturing and unsettling for the preacher.[6] The diverse perspectives these persons bring can also speak meaning to being for the preacher. The preacher will notice the ignored, be confronted by the uncomfortable, or find new empathy necessary for the sermon to accomplish its functions.

Most preaching-preparation processes conceive of the visual portions of preaching preparation as 90 percent of the sermon development process. This makes practicing the preaching life much more burdensome

---

5. After finishing this book's manuscript I was delighted to find Dave McClellan and Karen Marie McClellan's book *Preaching by Ear: Speaking God's Truth from the Inside Out* (Wooster, OH: Weaver Book Company, 2014). Preaching's premodern preparation patterns unsurprisingly fit Walter Ong's thesis as well as many pastors' personal current experience. Sermons are most often spoken to being, not written into being. Writing captures what speaking births.

6. So long as they know the preacher is safe, is truly seeking to learn, will not quote them without permission, and is not defensive.

and difficult to manage given the many pressures of life and ministry, particularly for bi-vocational ministers. There is great benefit in scheduling forced blocks of time for quiet reading, taking notes, reflecting, and beginning the sermon-crafting process with a pencil or text file. For these parts of the process a quiet set-aside space for scriptural study is nearly always best. However, reading the text out loud and listening to its resonance helps the passage "sound" forth. This way, during the process of reading, studying, taking notes, and sermon "scripting," the meaning of the passage continues to be discovered by the ear, the mind, and the heart of the preacher.

The Triple-Step Dance of Preaching

Preaching preparation is regularly described as a linear process moving through sequential steps ending in a sermon. This may be because exegetical processes in Western thought are more linear in nature, especially when a sermon is not in view. When a sermon is the end goal, however, the process is almost always more organic, cyclical, and unpredictable. The Eastern concept of a spiral is more helpful for sermonic preparation. Three larger moves guide the preacher through the preaching process, and speaking meaning to being helps each one: prayerful contemplation, scriptural meditation, and experimental expression.

First, *prayerful contemplation* is the least discussed move of preaching. It is assumed in many preaching textbooks, is a footnote in some, and is mentioned as a step in the process in others. The Johannine Christ reaches out to the preacher with the invitation to "Remain in me;" "I am the vine; you are the branches" (John 15:4-5). The preacher will find preaching preparation to be spiritually beneficial to the degree she is able to remain in attentiveness to and practice enjoyment of the presence of God. There is an inner conduit of the soul, an inner chamber of the heart, the tiniest of spiritual valves only the human is allowed to open. The Spirit will not force it open. When we hold this door ajar an inner communion with God brings peace and centeredness and produces fruit. Even if preachers do not formally pray, a continual attitude of prayer is like a steady ocean breeze on the working preacher's brow.

Including explicit prayer at multiple points in the process ensures multiple checkpoints for the preacher. A prayer for illumination before reading the text marks the process as prayerful from beginning to end. Breathing prayers or arrow prayers between readings helps the preacher to center, release anxiety, and initiate a receptive mode rather than strive for a sermon. These moments of spiritually focused pause often seem to be the spaces into which the sermon assembles in the mind as if a gift. The dead bones found in more focused study (second step in the dance) begin to come together in living form in the mind. A prayer journal related to the text and the sermon helps other preachers articulate thoughts as they emerge without fear of "getting it wrong." Verbal "conversing" with God can allow the preacher to express confusion and questions verbally and begin speaking meaning to being. When prayer consists primarily of requests for divine sermon help, prayer often becomes increasingly anxious with each successive hour. When prayer is centering, calming, and conversing in its tone, the sermon is free to come unexpectedly, as a surprise or a dawning.

Second, *scriptural meditation* is a repeated step in the sermon process. This meditation may look different in each succeeding phase of sermon study, but the basic function is the same. The preacher is wise to read multiple translations, pay attention to the logic and structure of the passage, do original language work, study the historical context, summarize the text's overall meaning, read critical commentaries, explore any literary features of the text, and so forth. Each of these movements of exegesis is best served by a continual inward openness that was initiated in more explicit moments of prayer. Otherwise the process becomes academic, distant, even detached from the person of the preacher, and finding a way to "own" the sermon later on is difficult. In many ways, homiletical exegesis is the most written about portion of the preaching-preparation process. The process is not always envisioned with space for meditation.

Thomas Long's eleven-step model of exegesis for preaching is the most used summary of biblical studies' insights for preaching.[7] Given its wide use and familiarity to preachers, a brief review should help ensure the preacher is including the most important points in the process each time. I. Get the text in view by (1) selecting the text, (2) reconsidering where the text begins and ends, and (3) establishing a reliable translation of the text. II. Get to know the text by (4) reading the text several times for basic understanding and (5) placing the text in its larger context. III. Attend to the text carefully by (6) listening attentively to the text through careful sincere questions and a search for genuine answers in the voice of the text. Remaining open for surprise from the text is crucial. IV. Test what is "heard in the text" by exploring the text (7) historically, (8) literarily (genre and convention), and (9) theologically.[8] Near the end of the exegesis process, the preacher (10) checks the commentaries. The first nine steps in the process require engagement with certain types of sources but not typically critical commentaries. Commentary engagement comes last so the preacher has a chance to discern the text for her people. She is the only one who has "one foot firmly planted in the text and the other foot firmly planted in the concrete circumstances of the hearers," and not the commentaries.[9] Finally, (11) the preacher summarizes the "claim" of the text on the hearers and the preacher in a single sentence summarizing what the text wants to say and do to the reader.

Long's well-worn and much-loved guide through the exegetical process for preaching has had one enduring suggestion from others. Prayer is an assumed reality for the preacher while the other elements of preaching preparation are not assumed. Cycling back to prayer in the midst of this exegetical process is important for the life-giving nature of practicing the preaching life. Remain in me, the gospel reminds us, for we are mere branches of the vine.

The third phase or step, *experimental expression*, turns the preaching process into multiple mini-rehearsals for the sermon in many forms. This

---

7. Thomas G. Long, *The Witness of Preaching* (Louisville, KY: Westminster John Knox Press, 2005), chap. 3.

8. Ibid., 88–94.

9. Ibid., 84.

suggests a second adjustment to Long's exegetical process—namely, regular breaks for experimental expression of discoveries in the text. Instead of religiously working through the eleven steps in order without shifting to other modes of inquiry, preachers can cycle through the triple-step dance of preaching throughout the exegetical process Long outlines so clearly. Prayerful contemplation, scriptural meditation, and then improvisational expression form a sermonic spiral of meaning making, not a single arrow or even a closed circle.

Some, who are characterized as "internal processors," do well through the traditional written forms of experimental expression. Note cards, legal pads, or freely written text files of various forms capture thoughts and move reflections toward expression in writing. If these written forms remain only visual, however, the move to the sermon is often stilted or delayed. The bridge from meaning to sermon is often difficult for preachers to cross, agonizing even, and fraught with anxiety because the meaning did not emerge in any verbal form. If the process is seamless and the writing moves directly into manuscript, almost universally the sermon sounds overly scripted, the presentation lacks life, and the experience of the sermon by the listener is a distant echo of the experience of the meaning by the preacher.

Experimental expressions of hunches, sermon sentences, and other ways of speaking meaning to being form a much less anxious bridge between meaning and sermon for the preacher. When speaking, the meaning is experimental and fragmented; Along the way the preacher is free to fail, free to be "heretical," free to question without answer, free to answer without apology, free to confront powers without fear, and free to discard previous thoughts for the sake of better ones. This freedom is part of what makes practicing the preaching life enjoyable rather than burdensome, liberating instead of trapping.

Speaking meaning to being, rather than only writing sermons into being, accomplishes something subtler and more powerful than improvisational interpretation. Think of the common counseling technique of asking a client to write a letter she does not intend to send to the person who wounded her. Tears come at times when writing the letter.

129

When the letter is read, to another human being, the speaker both hears it and experiences the process of expressing it to another. When this occurs, solitary tears turn to broken sobs. There is emotive power in speaking one's own meaning, hearing that meaning spoken aloud, while knowing another is listening.[10] When the first step of prayer has opened the inner awareness of God's presence to the preacher, experimental expression of the text's meaning is experienced by the preacher, and experienced as *heard* by God. This naturally brings the three-step dance back to the first motion: prayerful contemplation.

Speaking meaning to being is not restricted to private improvisational moments either. Both centered humility and compassionate empathy press a preacher to gain from others' perspectives (humility) and engage others' experiences (empathy). When experimental expressions of the in-process sermon are shared with others, there is greater opportunity for diverse viewpoints to emerge, for questions born of suffering to surface, or challenges to the unjust interpretation to be expressed. Preachers who seek out diverse conversation partners, such as preaching partners from varied theological traditions, or simply share their beginning ideas with those to whom they minister share the power of preaching and give members of the community a chance to respond before the sermon is publicly shared.

Turning this cycle or spiral of speaking meaning to being over and over in the sermon-preparation process accomplishes many good things. First, the preacher is able to stand under the sermon and hear its impact upon her own life. This humble stance of teachability infuses the sermon with authenticity, even questions the validity of the sermon that is only for others. Second, the preacher does not have to wait until the end of the exegetical process to concretize meaning or discover implications. Meaning is spoken to being as it emerges, keeping the meaning in its native tongue all along. There is no need to painfully translate the visual to the verbal at the end of the process. Third, the associations that come from speaking also allow the sermon to emerge more organically. Associative logic defines how humans speak. Structural logic often guides how writers

---

10. Hearing can be understood metaphorically for the hearing impaired preacher. Signing and following signs has much of the same experience for the signer and the conversation partner. The embodiment required by signing brings textual meaning into the heart language of the preacher.

write. When one thing leads to another verbally, the sermon is easier to follow for the listener, to remember for the preacher, and to recall later on for both.

Psychologists often speak of several different forms of memory. Rote memory versus logical memory is one distinction. Rote memory is the memorization of word-for-word, line-for-line exact placement of each piece in order in the mind. Preachers who memorize sermons in this way often sound stilted or forced. Unless they are extremely gifted actors, the listener experiences an inevitable loss of authenticity. The sermon does not feel "live." It is as if the preacher simply hit a play button. Logical memory, however, is the memory built on meaning and the association of meaning. It is analogous to the difference between memorizing directions to a person's house and knowing "the way" so well you can adapt to traffic.

Rote memory simply knows things in a specific order (i.e., three lefts and a right at the stop sign). Logical memory knows the reasons for any given order and can adapt to new circumstances without losing "the way." Just as important, associations lead from one idea to the next like landmarks in the mind. Preachers who develop sermons cycling through prayer, study, and expression end up knowing the way of the sermon. They have an ability to improvise and adjust to the moment. A lost word or a forgotten piece of data does not throw the preacher. She can arrive at the desired destination any number of ways, and few of those ways are unfamiliar or untested. Preaching by association, by meaning that leads verbally to the next meaning, is also easier for the listener to follow. Verbal communication nearly always works this way. In short, *when the sermon unfolds naturally according to the logic of association it is easier to remember because it makes more sense.*

Every preacher longs to practice what he or she preaches. Often, we simply do not give ourselves enough time to do so. When a preacher inquires of the passage, God, and herself "how can this change my life this week?" a crucial portion of preaching preparation begins. If this question can be tentatively answered nine or ten days before the delivery of the sermon, a new level of participatory wisdom has time to emerge. Living into the answer increases the intellectual and emotional energy of the preacher. Like a well-lit city on a hill at night, the living connection between the preacher and sermon is nearly impossible to hide if it is there. Perhaps just as important, when a living connection is there, preaching is more meaningful, more enjoyable, and more worshipful for the preacher.

Cycling the triple-step dance of preaching is an important concept for practicing the preaching life in sustainable ways. The call to the nursing home, the hospital, the prison, or the troubled home not only provides empathy and new contexts against which to test the sermon's compassion, but also "transition time" in which to pray, meditate, and express the sermon in new ways. The cycling of the triple step internalizes the sermon naturally into the preacher's intellectual, emotional, and spiritual life over the process so the sermon is a truly living sermon. Whether presented in manuscript, outline, or extemporaneous form, the sermon that is born by speaking and hearing carries with it the rhythms born of improvisation, the flow of natural speech, and the associated logic of verbal communication.

Often the first cycle through the three-step dance of preaching preparation requires the most disciplined motivation on the part of the preacher. A calendar appointment with enough time for prayer, focused reading of the text, and a few experimental expressions of its potential meeting will get the process started. The nonlinear nature of this repeating cycle does not mean the preacher can avoid planning study and sermon writing. On the contrary the sooner and more methodically a plan is devised, the more time the preacher will have for speaking meaning to being along the way.

In my experience with preachers, the bridge from the exegesis process to the sermon is not found best or most often by writing academic summaries of exegetical work. The "claim" of the sermon upon the listener and the preacher is *inductively* discovered and often experienced as a surprise in the midst of expression. When preachers give me summaries of the meaning of the text before they have spoken the text, the summaries rarely match what the sermon later becomes. Instead, I suggest preachers "try out" preaching sentences throughout the exegesis time both in written and oral forms. "Sounding" the sentences out tests whether or not the statements truly preach. Writing and then speaking for internal processors, or speaking and then writing for external processors, is the typical pattern. Both types of preachers need to sound it out so the meaning can be spoken to being. In keeping with Long's *Witness of Preaching* I suggest attempts at a focus sentence (what is the sermon saying), and a function sentence (what is the sermon doing to the listener). In addition, preachers are well served by attempts to craft a future sentence (the hoped-for change in the future).[11]

A self-designed sermon preparation process is the best way for preachers to stay disciplined in preaching preparation. This allows the preacher to use her own best practices and effective methods, while also keeping the preacher honest with any attempts to shortcut faithful study. Worksheets that guide the preacher step by step through faithful exegesis and a single-sheet master plan for which steps to follow in what order are helpful for preachers who need to know what to do next. The previous chapter provides a suggested rhythm for preaching preparation across four weeks. It is specifically designed to make the preaching life more manageable, less burdensome, and punctuated with orality. Through each successive step or set of steps prescribed in the previous chapter, the repeated three-step dance helps the preacher speak meaning to being again and again until a sermon is not only born but also brought to maturity. In this way, the preacher combines a linear habit with repeated cyclical moves toward meaning across time. This preaching process is both methodical and unpredictable, structured and free, visual and verbal, individual and communal, professional and spiritually alive.

For Reflection

1. How have you found the three-step dance of prayerful contemplation, scriptural meditation, and experimental expression already taking form in your own preaching preparation even accidentally?

---

11. Long, *Witness of Preaching*, 108. Long conceptually includes the hoped-for future change within his function statement. This conflates what the sermon enacts (*illocutionary*) with what the sermon effects in the future (*perlocutionary*) and often confuses beginning preachers as a result. The function in my view is what the sermon does to the listener during the sermon. The future sentence is a sentence describing the hoped-for change in the life of the listener and community as a result of the sermon.

2. How could you include the "three-step dance" of speaking to meaning throughout the process more intentionally? Rewrite your preaching preparation process designed in the last chapter to prompt the three-step dance in your next sermon preparation (prayerful contemplation, scriptural meditation, and experimental expression). Remember this can happen during "transition time" between pastoral duties.

3. Have there been times when your preaching seemed to resonate more with your own soul than others? In what ways has this chapter helped illuminate why those preaching seasons were more personally meaningful?

4. This chapter seeks to balance the tension between the freedom of oral expression and the precision of written expression. How can you find better ways to balance these two poles of excellent preaching?

5. Pick an upcoming sermon to develop. Write out a few tentative preaching sentences you think might express the focus (what the sermon is saying), function (what the sermon is doing to the listener), and future (the hoped-for change) of the sermon. Play with them out loud, alone, or by sharing them with a preaching partner. Change anything that does not fit the "ear." Then rewrite to better capture the spoken form rather than the written form.

CHAPTER 8
Giving Voice to Life

A snowstorm was falling around us. The snowstorm was real, the preacher merely spectral, and the eye felt the sad contrast in looking at him, and then out of the window behind him into the beautiful meteor of the snow. He had lived in vain. He had not one word intimating that he had laughed or wept, was married or in love, had been commended or cheated, or chagrined. If he had ever lived and acted, we were none the wiser for it. The capital secret of his profession, namely, to convert life into truth, he had not learned.[1]

This excerpt is perhaps the most quoted section of Emerson's writing for preaching literature. It is easy to forget Emerson was a preacher and a son of a preacher and was often described as a preaching philosopher. He could not shake the power of a sermonic mode even in his more public philosophy. Emerson goes on to say he does not condemn the preacher but pities him for he preaches "out of the memory, and not out of the soul."

Preachers who preach out of memory preach *about* the Word. Their sermons can be easily outlined, well written, carefully scripted spiritual speeches. Preachers who preach out of the soul proclaim a living Word. They speak from a living connection between the message and the messenger whether or not sermonic form, literary quality, or other rules of homiletics are followed. An electric current pulses from preacher through proclamation to the pew when preaching has soul. Preachers of memory

1. Ralph Waldo Emerson, *Nature Addresses & Lectures, Emerson's Complete Writings*, vol. 1 (New York: William H. Wise & Co., 1926), 137–38.

preach "what the church believes," not necessarily what the preacher questions, believes, or hopes. Preachers of memory preach memorized faith, old repentance, or re-gifted offerings. Preachers of soul proclaim fresh insight, recent wrestling, and their own sacrificial offering. We cannot claim to know the fullness of every passage each time we preach. Yet to preach without at least "tasting and seeing" in part is to miss one of the greatest joys of preaching. Even a glimpse of the promised land we have not yet entered is enough to give preaching its soul. Preachers need multiple ways of giving voice to life in their sermons to match the diversity of experiences they have with God and the scriptures. One tone of voice will not do.

Three Voices for Preaching

A common practice in older preaching books is to discuss the images for the preacher. Many of these metaphors or labels for the preacher (prophets, teachers, evangelists, and priests) speak primarily to the functions of preaching that particular sermons and personalities seek to accomplish (freeing, teaching, saving, or healing, respectively). It is true some sermons are prophetic, and there are people who primarily preach in prophetic ways. The same is true of didactic sermons and teaching-oriented preachers and so forth. Each of these could be pursued without naming the living connection between the soul of the preacher and the soul of the sermon.

Three metaphors have emerged over the last century tied to preaching voice rather than function: the herald, the witness, and testimony. For each of these ways of giving voice to life in preaching there is a unique way of relating the interior of the preacher to the heart of the sermon. There are also some key questions that will help the preacher relate to the text, others, the gospel, and implications for living well. By naming the level of living connection between the soul of the preacher and the soul of the sermon, the preacher accomplishes two things. First, she names the ways in which the good news relates to her in the current moment of her life. Second, she recognizes the room left for the good news to meet her even in the process of sermon writing or sermon delivery. This, of course, gives another reason to return to prayer.

The first voice is the herald (*keryx*). A herald preacher voices the sermon as an announcement of a divine message. Karl Barth claims we can never know the truth of a text through scientific, rational methods alone. The historical-critical method of biblical exegesis will not bring us to the point of being a herald.[2] A herald has received a message from the monarch, and a charge to announce the message has come with it. Prayer moves to the center as the preacher discerns God's announced Word through the written word. It is the announced Word the preacher proclaims and it comes through the scriptures, not merely from within them. In this way, the scriptures become the Word of God again for the preacher in God's timing and way.

It is easy to see how this vision for scriptural interpretation helps avoid preaching "from memory." The eventful nature of interpretation hangs on a Word breaking into the preacher's experience through engagement with the scriptures. Though the preacher studies the background and history of interpretation, he does not pass on mere background and history in the sermon. Though pieces of historical study may help root the announcement in the passage through which it emerged, the preacher really proclaims the announcement she experienced from the presence of God in her prayerful sermon-preparation process. The rootedness in the text, and the faith the Word will emerge through the word of the text, keeps this model of sermon preparation and delivery from becoming chaotic, personality driven, or given to private "revelations" for the preacher.

The herald's task is to make known and to present with authority born of personal knowledge. Presenting the message does not mean the preacher eliminates or conceals personal connection with the message. The herald derives her authority through the reception of the message from the monarch. The heralding preacher needs to receive something from God through the scriptures bearing divine authority. It is not enough

---

2. Mark A. Wallace summarizes Barth's view well describing a study of the language and context of the original text as a necessary "prolegomenon" or preparation for understanding, not understanding itself. See his "Karl Barth's Hermeneutic: A Way beyond the Impasse," *The Journal of Religion*, 68, no. 3 (July 1988): 399.

to study a passage until it is dissected, charted, and well understood as a literary analyst understands a poem. Something has been revealed to the preacher and the preacher is compelled to announce.

The herald metaphor is a worshipful, doxological, mode in announcing God's activity and implicating our response. The herald, or town crier, makes clear not only what God has declared but also how the townspeople can align their lives with the declaration. The worshipful preacher discerns the good news in God's announcement, experiences the good news in the announcement, and shares the good news as an invitation to response. Like Gladys Herdman in *The Best Christmas Pageant Ever*, the impulse of the herald's preaching is a press toward movement "Go on...he's over there! Go see him!"[3] Though the call to "go on...go see" is imperative in form, it is promise in tone. Christ is there, go and see.

Preachers who herald can move their scriptural study toward the voice of a sermon with a few key questions. In relationship to a text, preachers can ask, "What do I hear announced about the character and actions of God through this text? How is that announcement made new to me in this passage?" The characteristics, actions, and nature of God are explicitly stated, questioned, or implicated throughout the books of the Bible even when it has to be inferred. Asking this question keeps the attention of the preacher from turning merely to the anthropological (human help for human need) or historical (distant details about some other place and time). The focus is on God's nature, character, activity, and announcement of good news. Good news must actually be news—that is, a fresh insight born of textual study, prayer, communal engagement, and discernment of the way of God. I once assigned three different groups of preachers the same text for a preaching class. All thirty-six students preached beautifully unique sermons and each offered something *new to me*. It was a moving experience in the depth and breadth of scriptures as a resource for good *news* week after week, year after year.

The Spirit, the text, and the preacher are not the only parties involved. The preacher can also ask, "Am I missing portions of the announcement of the message others would hear?" One of the key weaknesses of the

---

3. Barbara Robinson, *The Best Christmas Pageant Ever* (New York: Samuel French, 1983).

herald voice is the individualistic image for interpretation. The pastoral authority of one individual separate from communal connection leads to a lack of humility and empathy. This can lead to delusions of wisdom and blindness toward injustice for the "Lone Ranger preacher."[4] Face-to-face interaction through practices of justice and compassion helps the preacher hear this "othered" word. As do diverse preaching partners. Part of what made the Herdman children's version of the play so attractive in the end is that the impoverished children heard with new ears and saw with fresh eyes. Othering the play caused the new, but truer, meaning to emerge: Mary was ragged and dirty, the divine child was burped as a human, the angel of the Lord caused a certain fear, and the wise men gave of the best they had to great personal sacrifice.

Once the preacher has "news" it must become good—gracious announcement of God's love for humanity in specific form. Preachers need to gospel people, not guilt them. It is not easy to discern why, but more often than not insight into scripture becomes "news" before it becomes "good." So the herald preacher asks, "How can this announcement be heard as *good* news?" In what way does this announcement make more possible what was once difficult, even impossible? How does the graciousness of God come through in the news of the message? If the announcement is rightly understood it will be rooted in and characterized by the love of God. It will create a new reality for the hearers through which they can live more loving lives. Preachers who announce a "try harder" ethic have not yet announced the good news of Christ.

Finally, the herald must ask, "How can life look if the message is embraced?" A herald who announces from a distance disregarding the effect it may have on people is not a beloved herald. A town crier comes from among the people, lives among the people, and receives the announcement as one of the people. Discerning the desirable possibilities for the future the message makes possible is key to the preaching life. Often the answer to this question ends up starting with "What if...?"

---

4. The Lone Ranger preacher is Justo Gónzalez's and Catherine Gonsalus Gónzalez's image for the private, privileged interpreter of scripture who does not listen to diverse others, effectively calling others "Tonto" with their actions if not with their words in *The Liberating Pulpit* (Nashville: Abingdon Press, 1994), 50.

"What would it be like…?" or "Can you imagine…?" There is no reason to share an announcement bearing no relevance to the people who hear it.

A preacher is often released from debilitating anxiety when she perceives herself as a herald. The authoritative decree, though softened with humility and compassion, clothes the preacher who has received from God with confidence. Rather than preaching her own word, which she doubts, she is preaching an announcement, a decree, a statement backed by God's present authority. Yet some cautionary tales are in order.

The pompous herald

His voice was sonorous, his diction dignified. He stood tall and straight-backed in the elevated pulpit. His authoritative demeanor impressed some. Others enjoyed his knowledge of doctrine and scriptural details. There were some honest souls after chapel, however, who shared things such as these, "It sounds like he's trying to be something he isn't: a radio personality or something." Another said, "*He* sure thought he was important." I knew the preacher. He was a gentle soul full of kindness and a generous spirit. His laughter was infectious, and his joy obvious—except when he entered the pulpit to preach.

When a preacher imagines himself "herald of the king," condescension can creep into the preacher's subconscious. Rather than seeking to be one of the people, the preacher seeks to stand tall above them and embody the aloofness of the announcing official. An officious, even pompous tone and demeanor can emerge. Particularly in cultures preferring flattened hierarchies this is an important cautionary tale. Avoid the stained-glass window voice, the two-syllable pronunciation of "Gawd-duh," or any preaching characterized only by *you* rather than *we*.

The partial herald

"I simply tell them what is true. I lay it out for them as clearly as I know how. If they reject it, that is up to them. If they do not 'feel' the sermon it is between them and God." This preacher went on to explain his ability to be stoic in the face of listener's inattention. It was as if all he shared could be summarized as, "If a simple straightforward explanation of the doctrine does not move them, nothing I can do will." This conversation with a preacher in the middle of a doctrinal series of preaching saddened me. There was communal feedback for his preaching that was a confirmation of his statements. Indeed, what he was doing moved the group as a whole very little. I think of him now as a partial herald. The data of doctrine is not the whole story. The emotive tone is clear in passages exclaiming things such as "my dear children" or "Onesimus my son...who is my very heart" or the prayer that the church will be able "to know the love of Christ that surpasses knowledge so that you may be filled to the measure of all the fullness of God" (1 John 2:1; Philemon 10 and 12; Ephesians 3:19 NIV). To proclaim the data of doctrine connected to these texts is to miss a major part of the proclamation. God's heralds are not like medieval heralds. We announce the loving, gracious heart of the divine. The announcement is "the master loves you to the point of death." What monarch, ancient or medieval, ever announced the same?

The judgmental herald

"They have to hear the bad news before they can ever appreciate the good news," she said to me in class. I replied to that overused aphorism with my belief that most people have already received the bad news. They have looked in the mirror and have seen themselves clearly enough. The class laughed; she did not. I left with the distinct impression her extended diatribes against the sins of others would continue no matter the feedback or consequences. The judgmental herald is so ever-present in some schools of preaching. The herald is not called to be judge. Any announcement under which others stand convicted, the herald does as well. If an announcement bears within it tragedy, it comes in the form of lament and is followed by the hope of grace. We are grieved by the conviction under which we stand and grieved for those who have not yet admitted the grief they submerge.

Preaching in the Voice of Witness

The second voice, the *witness*, is a more attractive version than the herald for many preachers. A herald announces the message she has received. A witness relays the experience of what she saw or heard. The witness softens the image of the herald, removes the positional authority, and elevates the necessity of personal engagement. A witness proclaims what she has seen and heard.[5] This puts the preacher in the mode of faithful recounting of the events witnessed. Whereas the herald seeks to discern a new announced Word, the witness seeks to experience the Word personally or through the lives of others. This voice for preaching is doxological insofar as it recounts what God has done and is doing in the tone of praise and gratitude.

Preachers who give voice to life as witness guide their preaching with some key questions. In relationship to a text, ask, "How does this passage bear witness to God's ongoing activity?" This presses the eventfulness of the scriptural witness. Studying "texts" often makes preachers feel like archaeologists, digging up boring dead bones of the past. This is necessary to a degree. Careful exegetical spadework is irreplaceable in preaching. The best archaeologist, though, is not interested in bones for bones' sake. Rather, she is looking for clues to the forms and ways of life bones, potsherds, and fragments reveal.

The witness wants to see again, hear again, experience anew the happening of God. Once this happening is discerned and lives vividly in the imagination of the preacher, he seeks to experience this happening in this time and place. This desire to witness a similar happening of God here and now leads the preacher to ask questions related to others: "How have diverse lives in our community experienced similar activities of God? Would others discern a different witness in the text?" A witness can recount what was overheard. A witness also stands at the edge of others' lives and experiences vicariously what is happening before her eyes.

Preaching others' stories is an art and a gift. It must be done with pastoral care, only with permission, and often with details and names changed to protect the person. These qualifications aside, voicing other life stories remains a powerful preaching practice. The listener wants to hear what God has done for others since it infuses faith for what God may

---

5. Thomas Long follows Paul Ricouer by uniting *witness* with *testimony*. I am using the terms differently to emphasize varying levels of connection between preacher and text.

do among us. The sermon not only gives the preacher a space to say what he wants to say but also gives the people who listen a chance to *hear* what they wish *they* could say.

Joy was a competitive athlete.[6] She repeatedly played through pain to achieve the championship dream she finally accomplished. On the last play of the championship game she won the game with a self-sacrificing play. She was paralyzed from the chest down. Months and months of tests, treatments, specialists, surgeons, and fifth opinions left her with the realization she would be paralyzed this way for life. Fed through a straw, she would be unable to sit or move except for some movement in her hands. Eighteen months later a preacher saw her lying outdoors on a quilt her mother made for her and, in a story that sounded like it was a new chapter in the book of Acts, asked if he could pray for her. She was in a community I have preached in many times. I know her relatives, her life-long friends, and many others who bore witness to her paralysis. In a few minutes following the prayer of the preacher she was standing, dancing, and calling out uninhibited praise. Whenever I hear her tell the story, I want to do the same.

I do not know why the healings that seem so prevalent in scripture seem so rare in my world. Some say they were simply myths bearing meaning. Others who rule out acts of God by definition doubt even the current stories that eyes of faith see and celebrate. Perhaps it is precisely that lack of belief that makes them so rare. Maybe we do not desire to see for others what we have not seen for ourselves. Yet Joy's story stands out so strongly I cannot deny something outside of the normal occurred. I cannot explain it and no longer feel the need to do so. I am a witness to her life and have heard the witness of those who knew her then.

When we preach from the resources of stories such as these our preaching bears the tone of witness. It does not have to be a dramatic restoration of health. We bear witness to the addict who tried every rehabilitation program and failed before coming to faith and finding wholeness. We bear

---

6. Joy Griffith has given me permission to share this small snippet of her beautiful life story. She lives in Atlanta, Georgia, and often shares her testimony in public ways. There are more personally impacting elements to this injury I will leave to Joy to tell. The short of it is, paralysis is not the only thing that was healed.

witness to the abused who found a new family—complete with parents, siblings, cousins, and crazy uncles—when she found the church. We bear witness to the refugee whose life was rescued by the people of God. We bear witness to the one to whom Christ appeared in a dream in a country where it is illegal to have such dreams. We bear witness to the spirit of peace in ecumenical dialogue. We bear witness when we see the love of God move people past racism, sexism, homophobia, classism, greed, gluttony, lust, rage, and other forms of broken humanity.

There is another way preaching in the tone of witness can infuse faith: bearing witness to the power of truly good news. To be a witness in the pulpit it is not enough to recount the events that happened back then, to those people, in that time. When we experience the good news, the text proclaims, we can say, "this did not just happen, it *happens*." Even in difficult, tragic texts, the good news can be witnessed. The key witness is not the tragedy in the story. The passages sometimes ever so subtly say, "This could have gone another way." Once we experience that other way and observe that way in others' lives it is natural to bear witness to it.

This leads to the gospel-focused question for the preacher as witness, "In what way can these happenings infuse faith and facilitate well-being?" Too much preaching assumes faith where there is doubt, presumes gratitude where there is cynicism, or takes commonality for granted where there is division. In every row, in every preaching moment, there are listeners whose faith is thin, cynicism strong, and sense of separation from God and the church very real. How can the happening the passage witnesses to, and the parallel happenings in the life of faith, now overcome these realities? How can they grace doubt with faith, gospel cynicism with hope, and overcome divisiveness with love?

Witnesses are cross-examined in court for many reasons, not the least of which is the possibility for misunderstanding. "How might the witness be misunderstood, misrepresented, rejected, or demeaned?" is a fruitful question to help qualify any sermon. Often another question given to a witness reveals the alternative meaning of the witness. On cross-examination, the witness's account convicted rather than acquitted, or cleared rather than blamed. Preachers must cross-examine the recorded witness of scripture to be sure they have not misunderstood or misrepresented the text. Many times, the broader context of the passage reveals the text cannot intend what was initially presumed. As I reread the story of the woman at the well, understanding gender roles and oppressive societal structures, the witness of the text seems to acquit her rather than condemn her. Many who cross-examine "there is no Jew nor Greek" discover, not the erasure of difference into blindness to it, but the radical inclusion of and awareness of it. Difference is named, embraced, and celebrated as "in" in the most comprehensive way.

The preacher must also allow her own witness to be cross-examined. How does this witness come across to diverse others? The more experienced and nuanced a preacher's empathetic imagination is, the more it will help the preacher. Yet it can only go so far. There is no replacement for others' perspectives on our witness. This is particularly true when we try to discern the ways in which our witness to the activities of God will be rejected or demeaned. It is better to realize the pain our broken witness may cause a widow or widower before we preach in front of many widows and widowers rather than after. It may be painful to hear how cynics would scoff or demean our witness before we give them a chance. Yet, once it is heard and understood the sermon can both validate and redirect cynicism at the same time. Often a single sentence can deflate the ability of a person to demean the witness we hold so dear. "I am not speaking of...; I am aware of...; You and I both know that...; We have all seen...and, it is unfortunately *still* true for many...; are all phrases useful for validating normal human questions and fears. Naming them often removes their power and releases the listener to move with the sermon.

Recently I listened as a preacher extolled the virtues of family. "We always come back to family," he said. He came from a very family-oriented culture, much more so than the majority culture in the room. The more he spoke of the "joy of being all together" and the "comfort we have" in those to whom we are related the more anxious I became. Because of my ministry to those there I knew some of the stories of abuse, abandonment, or even normal human disappointment in the room. The mental murals of their family tragedies still bore wet paint. Preaching before a holiday he seemed to be assuming everyone was looking forward to the obligation to return home. Most were not. Just as I almost decided this preacher was unaware of the difficulties of life, irrelevant to many of our situations, he simply said, "Now I know family can also be the absolute most difficult place for some to be." As the sermon turned I realized he knew the tension we felt, was ready for the pain in the room. We were ready to receive his witness.

The preacher bearing witness has a personal engagement with the activity of God that is deeper than the herald. When we can see current activity of God resonating with the scriptural witness, our witness bearing carries a weight it would not otherwise have. Listeners experience the difference between hearing someone talk about God and bear witness to the activity of God. This reduction of distance between proclaimer and proclaimed and between message and messenger is important. Yet some cautionary tales are in order.

The false witness

In recent years I edited a website featuring sermons from around the world. Repeatedly we found sermons with stories we loved told by people as if they were there when it happened, only to find the story was written by another preacher who was there when it occurred. At times entire sermons were delivered verbatim as if the preacher wrote them even though the file was easily found online. It is one thing to quote an insight from another, but it is another thing to state an insight as if it were your own. It is a third, and even more trust-damaging case, when a preacher proclaims someone else's story as if it were her own.

When a witness says he has seen what he has not seen, heard what he has not heard, witnessed what she has not witnessed, it is dangerous. There is a temptation among preachers to invent stories for the sake of effect. Whether it is out of desire to inspire, impress, or simply to fill empty space, the preacher can be tempted to be false in order to be loved. This is not an unfamiliar temptation to any human being. There is nothing wrong in telling a modern parable ("There once was a certain man..."), stories with details changed ("She was ten. I will call her Susan to protect her privacy..."), or even composite stories ("Have you not known many characters like this? It is a familiar play."), so long as it is clear to the listener when what is shared falls into these categories. What undercuts trust and belief is the preacher who shares a story as if it were his own, but it is not his own. This is false witness.

The uncertain witness

"I really cannot tell you whether or not God was involved in any active way that day. I wish I could." This sort of statement at the end of a powerful story in which eyes of faith see God's presence does not help the listener. It may help the preacher whose inner cynic is still alive and well. Yet it does not help the listener. It would be better to bear witness to what other witnesses have seen and heard than to undercut the witness we bring this day. Most listeners prefer the preacher who will simply state what he discerns God has done and is doing. So long as that discernment is fitting to the law of love, why should we cast shadows of doubt on dawning faith?

Preaching in the Voice of Testimony

The third tone of voice for preaching emphasized in recent preaching reflection is the voice of *testimony*. Testimony's mode of proclamation is engaged confession. The witness requires deeper personal engagement than the herald, but testimony exists on an entirely different plane. To testify is to proclaim what you have personally experienced. There is not an inch of remove between the soul of the preacher and the proclamation of the sermon. In the words of Anna Carter Florence, "Testimony gets us in the habit of standing in our own lives (as opposed to the lives we wish we had) and in the biblical text (as opposed to the world's texts), describing what we see (as opposed to what we wish we saw) and confessing what we believe (as opposed to what we should believe)."[7] The herald may say, "Hear the word of the Lord." The witness may say, "This is what I have

---

7. Anna Carter Florence, *Preaching as Testimony* (Louisville, KY: Westminster John Knox Press, 2007), xxviii.

seen and heard." The testimony says, "All I know is I was blind, but now I see," or, "I believe; help my unbelief."

Testimony is doxological in declaring the goodness of God in the biblical text and in personal experience of the life of faith. The preacher who can testify to the message proclaimed has levels of intellectual, emotional, and psychological energy connected to the sermon any other means cannot produce. Even when preachers do not use the first-person personal pronoun, listeners can sense when this energy hums underneath the words of the message. If the gospel has come as good news to the preacher, made its appearance in her life, then even bad news has foreshadowing of the good.

There are good questions to guide the preacher who preaches in the mode of testimony. First, in relation to scriptures, "How does the experience of God related through the text resonate with experiences of God in your life?" At times this resonance will seem immediate and direct. Matthew 25 resonated this way with Henri Nouwen who consistently saw the person of Christ in the faces of the "least of these." The inhabitants of Samaria resonate this way with my sister-in-law as she proclaims a message titled "Skipping Samaria." As an inner-city pastor, she has experienced people's tendency to skip Samaria over and over again. But she testifies to Christ's continual presence for her and those she loves in her own Samaria.

At other times, the resonance emerges over time as the passage unfolds its meaning to the preacher. Often the preacher experiences distance from the text at first. Resonance with the text comes only later once the gospel is seen through the veil of the textual details. Many weeks, a preacher will not be able to testify to the text at the beginning for the Spirit is using the text to bring a new utterance, a fresh gospeling of the preacher's soul. The freshness of the testimony may prevent it being shared directly for it is simply too personal, too fresh, too emotional. Still the energy of testimony is palpable as the preacher proclaims the truth he knows without explicitly sharing his story. Testimony is a tone of voice as much as a form of content. There is an unforced light in the eyes of the testifying preacher listeners can see.

In relation to others, preachers who wish to preach in the tone of testimony can ask, "What have others testified to in their experience of this text and life? How might others' stories better express what I have only experienced in part?" The witness may *only* see what has happened for others. The observed events lay claim to the witness, compel the witness, but do not emerge directly from his or her own experience. The one bringing testimony brings testimony true to her experience. Still, even when preaching comes as testimony, we must recognize the need for stories other than our own.

In relation to the gospel the testifying preacher can ask, "How can this passage bring good news to my own experience and then to the experience of others around me?" Recently a student of mine read the four texts from which she could choose to preach, and chose Zephaniah. A competitive athlete, she has a love for challenge like a quiet submerged fire within her. "Can any of you remember a sermon on Zephaniah?" she asked. Given the text we could see why we could not. God had decided to judge, and there would be destruction without reprieve. Where in this text is the good news? Eventually settling in on the word *wail*, she realized if the prophet believed God asked people to wail in advance, to mourn in advance, to be broken and contrite in advance, then God still believed someone might be listening. In the midst of hardened hearts and stopped-up ears, God expected a soul to receive what others rejected, to trust what others denied, to grieve what had not yet happened in faith. From her sermon emerged the gospel of lament. Sorrow was validated. Brokenness was cherished. Active, even proactive, grieving was affirmed.

Behind this young woman's story was a hidden energy. She spoke as one who had been through some minor version of an exile. I knew she experienced the prejudice of others because of her ethnicity. I also knew that, as an athlete, she had received a career-ending injury from which she battled back to play again—only to receive the same injury from which she would not recover. Underneath her affirmation of lament was a hidden sorrow, empathy born of personal pain, and wisdom that came from living the "wail" she was calling us to give. She did not just announce God's call to wail. Neither did she only bear witness to the suffering and wailing of others. Beneath the surface, the hum of the sermon's engine was her own discovery of comfort through the soul's wailing in the presence of God.

The following question will prevent a testimony from many sins: "How might your testimony be limited to your own experience or irrelevant to others?" For example, when a middle-class or wealthy preacher is speaking through the voice of testimony, I often am reminded of the great Langston Hughes poem "Mother to Son." The speaker of the poem is a mother addressing her son and begins this way: "Life for me ain't been no crystal stair."[8] The mother continues to describe the difficulty of the life she's lived in metaphorical terms. Her stairs have been splintery, sometimes bare, lacking luxury and comfort. During all of life's difficulties she can say, "I'se been a-climbin' on."

The testimony of the goodness of God coming from the preacher may simply ascribe to God the "blessings" of the personal benefits gained by others' impoverishment and pain. Preachers must be careful not to testify to the goodness of God without having an awareness of the struggling of others. Sharing the preacher's pain and struggles may cause a different frustration for the listener. Whatever pain and struggle the preacher has experienced and endured, listeners may have experienced more deeply and completely. We must be careful not to move too quickly from text through private meaning to testimony. As in all areas of preaching, humility, empathy, wisdom, and justice will increasingly guide the preacher to greater discernment of the right tone to strike.

Testimony is the most personal and therefore often the most irresistible form of proclamation. "I was blind but now I see" stands marble tall against all the rains of cynicism and doubt. A preacher's participation in the life of the gospel gives a kind of wisdom inaccessible to the uninvolved. The preacher's empathy for others' struggles is born not of mere random guess, but of broken hopes and secondary trauma. Testimony often provides an infusion of faith, hope, and love in the lives of listeners who have not seen but who long to hear that "the Lord is the everlasting God" who gives

---

8. Langston Hughes, "Mother to Son," in *The Collected Poems of Langston Hughes* (New York: Vintage Books, 1995), 30.

strength to the stumbling, comfort to the suffering, and raises up every soul who has all the time "been a-climbin' on."

The narcissistic testimony

As powerful as testimony can be, a few more cautionary tales are in order. The narcissistic testimony is often hard to define for a single sermon but easy to discern across time. When illustrations mirror the life of the pastor consistently across time it alienates people through shades of narcissism. Can a single person understand God as well as a married one? Can a person without children understand God? "When my kids were younger..." "My wife/husband and I..." "I love to run..." One of the interesting things about the three summations of Paul's sermons we have in the book of Acts is that none of them start with Paul. To the Jews, he began by recounting the story of the Jews. To the Greeks, he began with reflections on their understanding of gods and the unknown. To the rural community in Lystra who knew nothing of the Jewish story, cared little for Athenian pantheons, and lived lives close to the earth, Paul began with sun, wind, rain, and crops. Testimony in preaching should only rarely be the first word. In addition, preachers do well to avoid any story in which the preacher is the model or the hero.

One question that can help a preacher avoid narcissistic preaching is "Does this story in any way glorify me, the ministry with which I associate, or the church I lead?" Testifying to our glory, even if we say God helped us achieve it, makes it difficult to testify to the glory of God. This does not mean the preacher should avoid recognizing points of contact or resonance between her life and the sermon, or the church's life and the sermon. Sermons can gain life when the preacher keeps her testimony in mind (thereby gaining sermonic energy) while sharing another's testimony (avoiding narcissistic preaching). The line between raising a congregation's communal self-esteem and subtly elevating the self may be difficult to discern. Asking oneself difficult questions consistently goes a long way.

151

The sensationalist testimony

Sensationalist testimony is the use of shocking language or stories at the expense of accuracy in order to gain interest, move emotions, or impress the listener. After improvisational attempts to tell a story, or a free-writing session to try and capture it, ask some of the following questions: "Which is driving the use of this testimony more, my fear of being boring or the testimony's deep resonance with the scripture? Is there any language or detail I could describe as 'shocking'? If so, will the language or details detract from or add to the central focus and function of the sermon? Will the shocking elements be so memorable that other more important elements of the sermon be overshadowed?"

The exaggerated testimony

Exaggerated testimony is merely a subspecies of sensationalism. Ask an honest soul who exaggerates more, the preacher or the fisherman, and you might be surprised. Preachers and anglers both love to tell stories. Preachers and anglers are both prone to exaggeration. Because of this, the form of sensationalism we call exaggeration deserves focused attention. After improvisational attempts to tell a story, or a free-writing session to try and capture it, ask the following: "Are there any details I have inflated or removed in order to make it more impressive? Am I working hard to make God look better than God seems interested in looking?"

These qualifications for preaching in the voice of testimony are important. They should not be allowed to diminish the power of testimony in the mind of the preacher. Often the personal pronouns *I*, *me*, and *we* do not even need to be used for the tone of testimony to come through. A preacher can state, "God is a gracious and compassionate God to even the most sinful human being," with deep testimonial resonance without ever saying, "I was that human being." If a preacher can preach in the vocal tone of testimony, she should. As Karl Barth has said, "Our *may* is our *must*."[9] If a preacher cannot yet testify, he can bear witness to what he has seen and heard in the story of scripture and the lives of others. If a

---

9. Karl Barth, *The Church Dogmatics*, vol. 2, part 2, The Doctrine of God, trans. G. W. Bromiley, et. al., 1st edition paperback (New York: T&T Clark, 2004), 593.

preacher cannot yet bear witness, she can announce the good news of God in faith that if the master says it is so, it will be so.

Other Voices for Sermons

In order to help the pulpit gain life's energy and match life's diversity it is important the preacher not be the only voice heard. No matter how much a preacher seeks to avoid narcissistic preaching, if she is the sole voice heard Sunday after Sunday there is no way to avoid it. Imagine a preaching ministry in which you never know whose voice you will hear next. The steady voice of your shepherd remains, but you do not know whose testimony will stand as a living Word. When the preacher says, "Tom has agreed to share his experience," you lean in knowing you will be caught off guard and caught up in God's grace in others' lives.

Using others' testimonies in sermons does not always have to be done through the preacher's voice. Practical theologians have made the convincing case that saying *is* believing.[10] Articulating faith strengthens and clarifies faith. This means the practice of interviewing members of the congregation to help them share their stories of God's faithfulness forms their faith in the process. After all, speaking meaning to being helps the preacher. Why would the same not be true for the rest of the church or ministry?

Of course, concerns for what someone might say, past experiences of the cringe moment in the worship service, or a desire to keep the story within given time boundaries make this practice more difficult. With a little forethought and planning all of these concerns can be allayed through written, recorded, or guided interviews. Depending on the technical capacities of the pastor and the community, video editing can help a testimony achieve what you might call a biblical form. The stories we have in scripture often seem to be delivered in the most concise form

---

10. Amanda Drury, *Saying Is Believing: The Necessity of Testimony in Adolescent Spiritual Development* (Downers Grove, IL: IVP Academic, 2015). Drury's sources point to more than adolescent spiritual development though that is her field of interest. Human beings deepen and clarify faith when they articulate faith through signing, speaking, or writing.

possible. Paul's stoning and return to proclaim the gospel to the stoning community do not even take a page of scripture.

The embodied testimony of a person who is deeply respected by the community adds to the persuasive and moving power of the testimony. Sharing that person's story would not have the same effect. His embodiment reminds the community of his service, leadership, and faithfulness in ways mentioning them in a sermon will not do. There are other cases in which the embodiment of the testimony stands in stark contrast to the experience of the person's life. When a troubled child returns from the "far country" and testifies to the grace of God, the embodied testimony incarnates the gospel. In these cases, bearing witness to someone else's testimony would not have the same power as giving space for the person himself to testify. So long as the person is not coerced or used as a "medal" to show off in front of others, embodied testimony infuses faith and inspires celebration of God's goodness.

For many in a worshipping community, standing up in front of even a small congregation to give testimony to God's goodness is too much to ask. Video does not necessarily diminish the power of testimony. Depending on the skilled hand of the video editor, it can become even more powerful. The scattered testimony keeps its improvisational tone but gains the precision of edited speech. The person magnified on screen compels attention and draws in distracted listeners. Recorded testimonies can be used before, within, or following the sermon depending on where they best fit. Recorded videos can be vetted by a few easy rules: (1) The testimony should speak to the goodness of God in a way that resonates with many. (2) The testimony should resonate clearly with the message of the text and the function of the sermon. Otherwise it is just filling time or tugging heartstrings. (3) The testimony should be just long enough to tell the story, but not so long as to overtake the sermon. Anything more than one-fifth of the total sermon time is likely too much. (4) The testimony should be free from narcissistic tone, sensationalism, or awkward over-disclosure.

Pulpits can hum and pulse with the stuff of life. There is no reason for them to be cold, detached places where essays are read or exegetical notes shared. Good sermons riff off of the most beautiful themes of life. Great preachers speak as if they have not only something to say but also something to live. They announce a coming horizon they have seen, bear witness to a reality they have sensed, or testify to a vibrant life of faith. Giving voice to life, the best preachers bring to the pulpit an unforced, living voice.

For Reflection

1. Which of the three voices (herald, witness, or testimony) do you most often utilize in your sermons?

2. To share another's story is to bear witness. The interweaving of witness with testimony and heralding is part of the multi-vocal nature of preaching. A single sermon can live in all three voices. Think of examples of sermons in which you have heard this shift of tone or voice used with good effect.

3. Review the "cautionary tales" with each voice above (pompous herald, partial herald, false witness, narcissistic testimony, exaggerated testimony, and so forth). Which have you fallen prey to in recent preaching? If you are new to preaching, which are you more likely than others to fall into?

4. How might you weave together the voices of herald, witness, and testimony in an upcoming sermon?

5. What additional rules of art would you suggest for preachers for each of the tones or voices of preaching?

CHAPTER 9
Living Forms for Sermons

She nearly finished the to-do list on the back of the tithing envelope before he leaned over and whispered, "We are now beginning the second sermon," into her ear. The first twenty minutes of the sermon seemed an extended attempt to "gain attention" that was already there at the beginning. She had learned that if she mentally left the building at the beginning of the sermon, she could pay better attention at the end when the pastor seemed finally to get to what he wanted to say.

In another church, a young adult groaned the slightest of groans and covered it with a gentle clearing of his throat. The pastor just finished saying, "I want to explore this passage in three movements. First, I will..." The young man wrote on his bulletin, "Spoiler alert, I am about to bore you three ways to Sunday, watch me do it." His roommate smiled and wrote back, "I am going to give you three Christmas gifts. Let me tell you what they are going to be before you unwrap them."

"Well that was a beautiful homily," a father said to his daughter as they left the church building together. "Yeah, well written," she said. On the way home, there was a good deal of quiet in the car until she asked, "Can you tell me what to do with it though? I have no idea what that sermon means for me. Honestly, I never really do." He replied, "I do not know. I am sorry. Maybe it is time to visit a different church next week."

Every minister fears those thoughts run through listeners' minds. No minister wants those fears confirmed. These three stories are true; though I am paraphrasing the conversations I was not there to hear firsthand. In each, the preacher was working very hard, even too hard at times. All three messages fell far short of the ministers' hopes. Preaching left the listener discouraged for one reason or another. One preacher's sermons often seemed to be much ado about everything. The second was anticlimactic and lifeless. The third was a beautiful journey toward nowhere.

Whether a preacher tries to gain attention with raised voice and flailing arms or poetic prose and concise structures, listeners do not lean forward for every word falling from the preacher's mouth. In some preaching traditions preachers are not given many options for addressing the problem of listener attention. Often Evangelical or revivalist traditions only conceive of two cures: tell more stories or talk louder and faster. Many mainline or high church traditions conceive of two different cures: poetic prose or shorter sermons. Each would benefit from the other, to be sure.

On average, Evangelicals and preachers standing in the revivalist traditions need to narrow their vocal dynamics, control their gestures, and limit both the number and length of illustrative stories. The use of concise wording, imagistic metaphors, and shorter messages would benefit listeners greatly. No listener should regularly feel that he is now "entering the second sermon." Neither should the preacher be worn out from frantic pacing, wild gesturing, and voice-damaging histrionics. It puts off listeners more than it draws them in. There is another way to preach interesting and life-giving sermons without yelling and flailing the arms.

Many mainline and high church preachers need to widen their vocal dynamics, release their gestures, and make better use of illustrative stories in freeing ways. The use of impassioned appeals, expressive facial/vocal gestures, and stories that demonstrate portions of the good news would benefit their preaching greatly. No listener should have to ask in vain, "Now what do we do with that?" There is another way to preach interesting sermons without trying to become the next Robert Frost. Nor is limiting the sermon to the length of less than half a sitcom necessarily the best solution to listener disinterest.

In many ways the problem is confusion of preaching style and sermon form. *Preaching style* includes the following sermon elements and more: gestures, vocalization, use of stories, poetic metaphors, word choice, length, mode of delivery (manuscript, outline, extemporaneous), and the choice to conceal or reveal sermon structure. This is not an exhaustive set. To list all of the elements of style for preaching would take a book in and of itself.

Sermon form is made up of two components: structure and logical flow. Sermon form (structure plus logic) is often an underutilized force for listener engagement. Many preachers learn a form or two and then stick to them like glue. The conscious or subconscious thought is that the sermon form is not what makes the sermon living, but the content within it. Homileticians have learned over the last fifty years that form and content are to some degree inseparable. We communicate something by the structure and logical flow of our preaching. Preachers need living forms for sermons that speak meaning to being naturally, that flow from the preachers' struggles with God and the scriptures.

Sermon logic addresses the underlying flow of the sermon unifying all its moves and structures.[1] Think of it as the current underneath the surface of the ocean. The surface may be broken into waves through peaks and valleys, but the current underneath is a steady movement in a clear direction. Sermon structure determines the shape or structure of the sermon on its surface. Far from superficial, the size and spacing of waves determine the experience of those on the surface significantly. The current determines direction. The structure defines order and rhythm. The two together determine sermon form.

It is tempting to think one particular "style" is a preacher's personal preaching identity. As a result, preachers do not vary their preaching dynamics or adjust dramatically enough to the feedback they receive. After all, a change in style feels like a change in preaching identity. We do not want to be "inauthentic." Preachers also long to hold the attention of the listener. The sermon logic is invisible to many preachers. As a result, rather than adjusting the current of the sermon (sermon logic) to create

---

1. David Buttrick's *Homiletic: Moves and Structures* (Philadelphia: Fortress Press, 1987) presses preachers to make the "logic of movement" in a sermon travel in ways "natural to human consciousness," p. 310. Sermons are not just bullet points on the page, content statements to be "unpacked." They are logical "moves" from one thought to another held together by a discernible structure that unfolds in the listener's mind. A move then is a sermonic progression. A structure is the way the moves are interconnected to create the sermon "form." The moves gain their "movement" through the logic that flows underneath them.

irresistible movement, the preacher exaggerates the chosen style. What most preaching books call "form" sometimes ignores the underlying logic and only provides the preacher with a *structure* that is called a sermon form. At other times the logic and the structure are equated so closely that we talk of "inductive forms" when in reality many forms can be used deductively or inductively.[2]

Sermon logic is the greatest force available to preaching for holding the listener's attention. When the sermon logic is strong, the structure and style can be weak and the sermon will still carry the listener in the right direction. Thinking of sermon logic helps the preacher pay attention to the underlying, seemingly invisible nature of preaching. How does the sermon move? What current is driving each section of the sermon forward like waves heading to shore?

Eugene Lowry's *Homiletical Plot* is one of the best texts for understanding sermon logic. Though the "Lowry loop" is often described as a form, it is best understood as exploration of sermon logic. Based on Aristotelian descriptions of plot, Lowry works to describe the invisible plot-like logic that flows under all good sermons. Lowry's primary point claims psychological tension is what holds listeners' attention and keeps them moving along with the sermon. Some form of ambiguity, conflict, or tension broadly understood is required at the outset of the sermon. The complication of the ambiguity helps to diagnose the connection between the scriptures and life in meaningful and authentic ways. From within the voice of the text comes the clue to resolution, a clue to the good news of God. When this clue is extended into life, the listener experiences the good news. When that experience is directed toward the rest of life, the listener can anticipate the consequences of living according to that good news, or choose to ignore it. The sermon logic, its deep current, then moves from some form of tension, through a deeper diagnosis of that tension, to a clue that turns the tension toward resolution, through an experience of the good news, to an anticipation of the future lived according to the good news.

---

2. Deductive sermon logic moves from claim to support, doctrine to scriptural data, pastoral guidance to illustration, and so forth. Inductive sermon logic moves from question to answer, problem to solution, or conflict to resolution.

When a preacher is unaware of this current she will not understand why one sermon seems to flow so easily and interestingly while another sermon feels as though it is one untimely born.

The key element of Lowry's plot-based preaching logic is the tension maintained in the listener. All of the following sermon logics are ways of exploring tension: question to answer, problem to solution, ambiguity to clarity, disbelief to belief, cultural truth to gospel truth, or conflict to resolution. These are examples of *inductive* sermon logic. Inductive sermon logic moves from data to conclusion, question to answer, problem to solution, or from particulars to a general truth. Lowry, along with all members of the New Homiletic, see inductive sermons as the way to rescue preaching from disinterest.[3] This can be true, especially if the logic and the structure work hand in hand to produce a living form. This chapter outlines Lowry's suggested structure below. But of greater importance than the form is the tension he suggests we discern and maintain in sermons. Inductive logical flow can be just as boring as deductive flow when the tension is forced, false, or feeble. Imagine a sermon starting this way, "Who were the Jebusites?" It is a question. It is moving toward an answer. However, the vast majority of listeners will feel little tension with the sermon unless it is developed and directed to "scratch where they itch."[4]

Deductive sermon logic moves from statement to support, solution to explanation, proposals to argumentation. Deductive sermons can also maintain a tension within the sermon logic when the deductive claim, proposal, or statement inherently creates tension within the listener. White Western preaching often misses this reality when majority world and minority Western cultures consistently produce preachers who preach deductively to growing worshipping communities of faithful disciples. Deductive sermons are not dead in today's world. *Boring*

---

3. The New Homiletic is the description given to a group of homileticians who sought to devise a new way for sermons to communicate to modern culture in the late twentieth century. For an introduction to and renewal of the New Homiletic's insights see *The Renewed Homiletic*, ed. O. Wesley Allen Jr., (Minneapolis: Fortress Press, 2010).

4. Eugene Lowry, *The Homiletical Plot: The Sermon as Narrative Art Form*, expanded edition (Louisville, KY: Westminster John Knox Press, 2001), 19. Scratching where the listener itches is Lowry's way of describing the current, or logic, of the sermon. The weakness of this model in the wrong hands is a turn to a highly anthropological focus. God is eventually shaped in the reverse image of human questions and human needs.

deductive sermons are dead. If the tension is there *for the listener* in a way that touches their deepest felt concerns, deductive logic will be interesting. I remember when my friend and colleague preached a sermon titled, and that began with, the sentence "God is never enough." It was a deductive claim. But it upset the apple cart, to use Lowry's phrase, introduced tension, and had both skeptic and saint leaning in to see where this sermon could possibly go.

This is important for the preacher to understand if she wants to preach living sermons with living forms. The logic of the sermon can be conceived as the directional current of the sermon. That current is usually deductive or inductive as a whole and may switch between inductive and deductive between differing moves. The key to sermonic interest is not whether the sermon is inductive or deductive, but whether the sermon's current is strong or weak.

How does a preacher find a strong current for a sermon? A lack of preaching virtue is often the block to discovery of sermon logic. The preacher lacking in humility does not need to find anything new; he only needs to find good ways to say what he already knows. As a result, there is no tension for the preacher, no ambiguity, no conflict. This comes through in a message in which the sermon does not wrestle with God or with faith, but presents it as a matter of accepted fact or rejected myth. The predetermined nature of the sermon fails to hold attention. One source of sermonic tension is centered humility. The humility to face our own struggles with God, confusion about theology, even resistance to living the Christian life provide rich resources for preaching tension whether or not we mention our own wrestling in the pulpit. It comes through. Name your own questions. Write down your struggles. Announce your doubt to the sky. When a passage troubles the waters of your soul, force yourself to get up and get into the waters yourself.

The preacher lacking in compassionate empathy does not realize the tension others feel with scriptural and theological truths. When the real suffering of others is hidden to the preacher, it is often difficult to discern a tension that will live within the listener. The preacher may discuss a question no one is asking, solve a problem few are facing, or clarify an ambiguity no one is feeling. At other times the tension is too great, and the preacher without empathy ignores it. Like a power line weighed down with icy limbs, the connection in between the preacher and listener breaks from the strain. I will never forget my friend's first Sunday back in church after his wife succumbed to a long battle with lung cancer. He picked up the bulletin, saw the sermon title "All Things Work Together for Good," gathered his children, and walked back out the door. Take time to walk through the hallways of memory. See the suffering faces you have comforted. Ask God how this passage could be true for them. Speak to those in more difficult life circumstances than you. Lay their lives like a lens over the passage and see what is suddenly highlighted.

The preacher lacking in participatory wisdom may give a shallow diagnosis of human conditions and the meanings of the passage. Because the preacher has not yet engaged her life deeply in the matter of the message, the tension she creates is weak or superficial. The sermon takes on the form of a wiki page with easy steps, shallow bumper stickers, and unsatisfactory guidance. It is difficult to help others face their demons when we have not faced our own, or to help others lift shame while our own weighs us down. Do not give an abstract diagnosis of humans in general first. Instead, allow the meaning of the text to deeply diagnose your own soul. Name your disease. Then discover a particular gospel—that is, the gospel for your own soul. Prescribe your medicine. Even if the treatment plan will be long, begin its course today. Even if the education of the soul will take time, sign up for the first class. Then, and not until then, can you draw a diagnosis and deeper cure for others. Again, this does not mean we cannot preach what we have not mastered. We are not Donatists. Still, preaching is better when we have tasted what we serve.

The preacher lacking in courageous justice may miss the tension altogether. If the world already seems just and fair, or as just and fair as it needs to become for now, then texts proclaiming justice will sound hollow or become over-spiritualized. The tension between "now" and "not yet" disappears. Genuine interest devolves into self-righteous head nodding. Scriptures speak of not harvesting the boundaries, and the preacher speaks of having healthy margins. Scriptures speak of welcoming the stranger, and the preacher talks about having church people over for dinner. Jesus says to do good for the least of these, and the preacher asks us to send some encouragement notes to stressed-out acquaintances. If courageous justice is weak or missing, the passage's real tension with our lives is submerged or silenced. Often our own attempts to procrastinate or domesticate doing justice are what takes away the prophetic edge a sermon could otherwise have. Allow the passage to press you to uncomfortable places. What risk would it have you take on others' behalf? When we put ourselves at risk the tension we feel helps give rise to the parallel tension most likely to underlie the sermon. It may not be the same tension, but it will be a cousin to it.

Preachers who give wonderfully interesting sermons start by being deeply interested people. Often this interest emerges as a hunch, a question, or the barest beginning of inspiration. Preachers can allow this beginning germ of a sermonic idea space to emerge through improvisational preaching, communal discussion, free writing, and other forms of experimental expression. Given enough time, these experimental expressions (speaking meaning to being) will become a well-constructed house in which the sermon can exist. This is the great insight of Fred Craddock's sermon journey. He desired preachers to recreate a journey with the text, parallel to though not identical with the journey the preacher experienced. This focused sermon development on the underlying unifying current of the sermon—that is, the sermon logic.

With experience preachers become more adept at developing the underpinning logic or strengthening the invisible current of the sermon. Yet even experienced preachers often find great improvement in their preaching by refocusing intentional effort on the flow of the sermon's logic. The logic of the sermon is what holds the "what" together with the "why" and the "how" the sermon seeks to proclaim. The various types of sermonic logic all make more particular the general truth of tension or suspense in the sermon. These types include problem/solution, question/answer, disbelief/faith, cynicism/hope, confusion/clarity, uncertainty/confidence, difficult statement/eventual acceptance, old doctrine/contemporary significance, and so forth.

Some questions help preachers draw this logic to the fore. Does the action or description of God somehow surprise us in this passage? Is there anything implied about God that is troubling? What human need does this passage seem to articulate, infer, or relate to? What human condition mentioned or inferred in the text blocks the need from being fulfilled? How does God relate to this human need in the perspective of the passage? What is the tension between the human condition and divine nature/activity? Over time these questions become answered automatically in the sermon-preparation process out of habit. When these questions are answered a suspense between reality and possibility emerges. The reality of human life is more carefully diagnosed. Even inspiring elements create tension because they inherently create tension between who we are and who we are inspired to become.

Much of the above points to one central truth. The reality of human life requires the participation of the preacher in the Christian life in order to discern. The more deeply that participation has taken the preacher, the more insight the preacher will have to offer. The possibility opened up by divine activity or promise is more carefully examined. The participation of the preacher in the Christian life also helps the preacher discern the subtleties of divine activity and promise, the diversity of human perspective on those possibilities, and the reasons human beings often choose current reality over divine possibility.

Point-Based Sermon Forms

Many preachers find the practice of the preaching life overly burdensome. For them, the challenge to put together meaningful thoughts into organized sermonic form is like trying to nail down a cloud. For other preachers, the practice of the preaching life can become somewhat tedious. Like any other often-repeated task, it can take on rote form, like always driving the same route to work each and every day. Automatic pilot takes over. When a preacher starts sermons the same way, ends them the same way, and moves through them the same way week after week, even the preacher can become bored. Sermon form can help the anxious preacher put hedges around the cloud and the bored preacher go home by another way.

Point-based sermons have had a long history in preaching. Point-based sermons are often based on what homileticians call a "cognitive propositional" model of truth. This model perceives of truth as discrete sets of concepts or propositions that can be conveyed in words and understood intellectually. The clearly written point proposes the concept in cognitively clear ways. There has been much critique of cognitive propositional models of truth.[5] The critiques boil down to the simple fact there is more to truth than propositions. A purpled sunset cannot be bound up in a set of bullet points. This does not mean points are evil or useless. After all, even these critiques are typically communicated, at least in part, as propositions. The following are a few examples of point-based sermon forms that help connect the structure of the sermon to the underlying logic or tension of the sermon so that the points come to life.

Hegelian synthesis

This sermon form is a simplified version of the synthesis usually ascribed to Hegel: thesis, antithesis, synthesis.[6] The first point is a thesis presented as if it were true. Typically, the tension underlying the sermon is a conflict with the passage or a difficulty with the thesis for the lives of real people. This tension is often unstated at the beginning but felt in the listener. The preacher transitions to questioning the first thesis giving voice to the tension felt within the listener. As the conflict emerges between the two (thesis and antithesis), space is made for a new hearing of the text and its good news. The synthesis does not decide between the first two options. Instead it rises above them both, including elements of each, to a new thesis that overcomes the conflict. This sermon form can be complicated for more difficult concepts to cycle this way: thesis, antithesis, thesis, antithesis, and then synthesis.

---

5. For one homiletician who critiques this model of Charles L. Campbell, *Preaching Jesus: The New Directions for Homiletics in Hans Frei's Postliberal Theology* (Eugene, OR: Wipf and Stock, 2006), 141. I am inclined to integrate the critique with a more thoughtful use of propositions.

6. Samuel D. Proctor, *The Certain Sound of the Trumpet* (Valley Forge, PA: Judson Press, 1994).

Agree, deepen, correct

This sermon form starts with a concept that is agreed upon by most in the worshipping community. Though there may be a few outliers, the first concept presented is one all can agree upon. Stating this agreement gives voice to the community. It also helps unify the community on the basis of shared beliefs. This first point is quickly presented and only briefly illustrated. The tension is usually introduced subtly with phrases such as *there is one thing on which I think most of us can agree.* The sermon then deepens the agreed-upon statement with a more complex understanding of the same concept. Often the sermon has only one singular move within the "agree" section. It then has multiple sub-points within the "deepen" section. The twist and conclusion of the sermon, "correct," comes in the form of correction to life or belief built upon deeper understanding.

Rhetorical ladder sermon

A well-established rhetorical form for public speeches is often called the "ladder" speech. It is conceptually similar to the previous form but different in the number of moves and form of progression. It is called a ladder since it begins with lower-level concepts that are resting on more solid ground between the preacher and the listener. Something as simple as "God is love" might be a beginning concept. The ladder then moves logically from one "rung" or point to the next (God is superabundant love) gradually ascending to more controversial or difficult-to-accept truths. Rather than deepen the first, it takes the sermon into an ascending direction. "We are all strangers and aliens in the world of God's love" might be the second or third rung of the ladder. "God's love is particularly focused on immigrants and refugees" could be the third or fourth rung. "Immigration is a hotly debated political issue" might be the fifth, and "Making immigrants feel at home is a faith and love issue" could be the sixth. By moving from least difficult to receive to most difficult to receive, the preacher makes it more likely for the listener to complete the sermon journey and hear the just word.

167

Inductive Sermon Forms

Sermons of nearly any form can flow in inductive ways. There are, though, sermon forms created to be inductive by the nature of their structure. The first three of these were designed by preachers and professors of preaching to help ministers discover sermons and structure them in the same process: the Craddock journey, the Lowry loop, and the four-page sermon.

The Craddock journey

Fred Craddock asks the preacher to recreate for the listener the journey toward the sermon she experienced herself.[7] Of course a sermon that lasts less than half an hour is not enough time to fully recreate a sermon-preparation process lasting eight hours. The broad movements of the process turn into the broad movements of the sermon. This "form" then is the least structured in advance of all the forms in this chapter. Very often the sermon moves in something close to the following way because of the nature of a sermon journey: an initial reaction to or sense of the passage's meaning, a point of contact with lived experience, a shift in meaning caused by closer reading of the text, a question or problem that emerges from the shift in meaning, a diagnosis of human existence based on the new meaning, the good news in the passage, imagistic depictions of the good news in current life, a benediction that hands the sermon to the listener. This form is really the replication of a process. As a result, it is unpredictable to a degree. The common features recognizable in the sermon form are listener participation in the circle of interpretation, description of earlier interpretations *as if* they were the sermon's point, shifts in sermon direction that mirror the pastor's sermon journey, and a handing of the sermon to the listener at the end to "complete" within their own lives.

The Lowry loop

The Lowry loop is one of the most well-used, well-loved, and misunderstood sermon forms.[8] It is named a "loop" because the sermon takes an immediate turn downward in increasing tension toward a gospel "turn" at

---

7. Fred B. Craddock, *As One without Authority*, 4th ed. (St. Louis: Chalice Press, 2001), 116.

8. Eugene Lowry, *The Homiletical Plot: The Sermon as Narrative Art Form*, rev. ed. (Louisville, KY: Westminster John Knox Press, 2005).

the bottom of the loop. Then rising upward the sermon continues to explore and experience the good news of the text in the lives of the listeners, forming a "loop" with the introduction, like two ends of a rope lying across each other. Unlike Craddock, Lowry is not describing a sermon-preparation process exactly. Though the Lowry loop will stick easily in the mind of the preacher as she works on sermon development, the first portions of sermon preparation do not map as easily into Lowry's method as Craddock's.

The sermon form consists of five movements intended to unfold naturally into a seamless sermon plot: (1) Upset the equilibrium (oops). Listeners have reached a status quo with scripture, God, and life. In order to be changed, that status quo has to be shaken by some ambiguity, question, problem, or tension. The tension should emerge naturally from the passage and be central enough for the passage and the listener to guide the entire sermon. (2) Analyze the discrepancy (ugh). This complication of the plot requires things to get worse (head down in the loop) before they get better. The preacher uses textual analysis and diagnosis of the human condition together to deepen the sermon. (3) Disclose the clue to resolution (aha). This is the turn of the sermon paralleling the preacher's discernment of a turn in the passage. How can the gospel begin to teach, heal, save, and liberate the listener in a way that is good news? (4) Experience the gospel—whee! In this section the function of the sermon is enacted on the listener as the gospel introduced as a clue unfolds into an experience of the goodness of God. The intellectual exposition moves into emotive implications heading upward in the "loop." (5) Anticipate the future (yeah). The intellectual and emotive now move into volitional (the will) engagement of the listener. Instead of creating a push from behind, however, the sermon creates desire by painting a picture of a desired future the gospel could help create. Oops, ugh, aha, wee, and yeah is the shorthand version of the form.

The four-page sermon

Paul Scott Wilson developed this inventive sermonic process and sermon form.[9] The four pages are easy to remember, though not as easy to

---

9. Paul Scott Wilson's book has been revised and updated. See *The Four Pages of the Sermon: A Guide to Biblical Preaching* (Nashville: Abingdon Press, 2018). The pages Wilson mentions are metaphorical references to a theological stance the preacher is taking. The length is flexible given the context and available time.

master. (1) Trouble in the text. Like the first two narrative sermon forms, the preacher's journey through the circle of interpretation helps define one of the first components of the form. Page one is filled with exploration of a conflict within, problem surrounding, or a question emerging from a close reading of the scriptural passage. (2) Trouble in the world. The preacher discerns a conflict, problem, or question in the world that resonates with the first page. Current-day, contextualized depiction of life fills the second page. Like Craddock and Lowry this theological diagnosis of the human condition is key to the success of the sermon. (3) God's action/good news in the text. The scripture is interpreted not merely in a phrase-by-phrase "unpacking." Instead, an explicit search for the good news guides exposition from beginning to end. The discovery of this good news is explored on *page 3* as it brings beginning resolution to the trouble in the text. (4) God's action/good news in the world. In this page the good news in biblical passages is extended into transformed life in the world. The effects of the gospel are imagined, illustrated, even initiated into the life of the listener on *page 4*. Though Wilson consistently uses a cinematic metaphor for the process, many preachers simply follow the method of the pages and miss the imagistic and narrative underpinnings of the form. These four pages are written in whatever order they are discerned. Then the four pages can be shuffled in any way that best fits the preacher's sense of how the sermon should unfold.[10]

The next three sermon forms are explicitly inductive in form but are not as deeply connected to individual homileticians.

"Not this, not this, but that."

This simple sermon form mirrors three-point sermons in the pleasing and simple structure of three moves. However, unlike most point-based sermons, the first two points are not what the sermon intends to say. It also does not necessarily follow the Hegelian model. It simply states two things people might think based on the passage and their experience of life. Each of

---

10. Depending on single or double spacing and other formatting issues, one benefit of this sermon form is the creation of a beginning script that fits closely to typical sermon lengths. Of course the concept of a "page" is flexible. For contexts expecting longer sermons each page may be single spaced or even more than one "page."

these is explained away through deeper analysis of the text and exploration of life. The final move is to explain what *is* the good news in the passage, what is the liberating truth in life. This sermon form can be extended to three or four "not this" moves but should rarely extend beyond. Five major moves in a sermon is generally the length a sermon can withstand.

Narrative recounting

This sermon form takes a narrative in scripture and imaginatively immerses the listener into the story. The historical background, intertextual study, and imaginative reading of the preacher help the story become a world in which the listener lives for the sermon. The plot of the story in the passage becomes the structure of the sermon generally speaking. This can be a very powerful form for narrative passages in which the story seems to speak for itself. Parables can be reconstructed this way as well as historical passages. The preacher has to be careful to make it clear when greater imagination is being used in order to read between the lines. Phrases such as *I imagine it was*...or *I wonder if*...help the sermon narrative expand without leaving the listener in disbelief. Implications of the narrative are typically unfolded along the way and gathered together at the end through a conclusion fitting to the story's end.

Dual narrative

"I want to tell you the same story twice, separated by two thousand years," is how the sermon began. The first character is the rich fool discovered in the middle of the best harvest year of his life. Through flashbacks the historical background of this farmer's presumed life is imaginatively filled in. Then a construction worker named Mike is introduced when he first meets his wife. Their life of struggle to "make it" brings him through success to the point of a devastating piece of news. The farmer in the story is revealed to be in his last day. Mike then is revealed to face terminal illness on the day he sells the business to retire young. In both cases, the life "hoped for" was all too easily lost before it was ever enjoyed. The intertwining of these stories allows the biblical story and current forms of life to maintain their integrity but to deeply resonate with each other. Helping the listener identify with several different characters in diverse cultures and times reenacts the power of the parable.

This sermon form acts like a playing of a fifth interval on the piano. The perfect fifth is the most stable-sounding interval other than unison, or an octave. The differences between the stories create enough contrast to add texture and meaning. They resonate well enough together to create harmony, beauty, a "fitting" feeling. The imaginative retelling of the biblical narrative helps the story gain a new hearing. Often the story is not revealed at the beginning of the sermon, but slowly it dawns on the listener as "familiar" and then finally as biblical. The contemporary narrative is the other note in the simple cord. The better the story is crafted or told, the more points of resonance there will be with the biblical narrative retold. If the story is too different, it will feel like the preacher struck a "wrong note." If the story is too similar, it will feel flat and too simplistic. It is important to make the biblical story the "dominant" chord and the contemporary parable or story the "tonic" chord. Once the preacher has the feel of this form it is a powerful sermon form to use sparingly.

Move-Based Sermon Forms

The daisy refrain

A daisy refrain sermon begins and returns to a central sermonic statement or question at the center of the "flower." The sermon then moves outward from the statement or question and returns to it, giving the center new meaning and beauty each time. Each move out from and back to the central refrain or question forms a petal. One of my students recently preached a sermon in this form. The sermon began with the question, "Has anything taught you to count your days well?" It was, of course, a sermon on the psalm whose prayer expresses the brevity of life. The sermon moved backward and forward between personal testimony of a life-altering crisis, exposition of the passage, imaginative empathy with the author of the passage, theological reflection, stories of others' lives in suffering, and ways of facing weakness and mortality in meaningful ways. Between each major move the preacher asked us, "Has anything taught you to count your days well?" When the sermon ended, the counting of days was clearly the focus and the question bore deep intellectual, emotive, and spiritual meaning for the listeners. Care must be taken to ensure the center of the flower emerges from the central focus of the passage. The number of moves should also be limited so that the sermon does not become too long, nor does the central refrain become irritatingly repetitious.

Moves to celebration

Henry Mitchell's seminal work *Black Preaching* and Frank Thomas's *They Like to Never Quit Praisin' God* outline components of sermons whose moves end in celebration.[11] This great stylistic contribution to preaching theory by African American preaching is often summarized in the following colloquial set of moves: start low, continue slow, rise up higher, catch on fire, sit down in the storm.[12] These "moves," however, describe the *style* of the moves not the logic, content, or even the structure. Early movements start in somber or serious tones and deal with reality as it is or the text as it seems on the surface. Often some portion of the sermon offers a form of lament, giving voice to the suffering and sorrow of the human condition.[13] With each successive sermonic move the sermon builds toward God's redemptive acts on behalf of the people of God. God's intervention in the life of the oppressed is central and is the generative reason of the good news. The good news is then explored in directly applicable ways. It is declared as "still true," or true yet again, in ways that engender praise,

---

11. Henry H. Mitchell, *Black Preaching: The Recovery of a Powerful Art* (Nashville: Abingdon Press, 2010). Frank Anthony Thomas, *They Like to Never Quit Praisin' God*, revised and updated version (Cleveland, OH: Pilgrim Press, 2013).

12. Cleophus LaRue believes the distinctive power of African American preaching moves beyond stylistic concerns to its deeper hermeneutic. African American preaching's style emerges from generations of suffering, but also from generations of faith in a "God of infinite power who can be trusted to act on their behalf" (*More Power in the Pulpit: How America's Most Effective Black Preachers Prepare Their Sermons* (Louisville, KY: Westminster John Knox Press, 2009), 2–3.

13. Luke Powery's *Dem Dry Bones: Preaching, Death, and Hope* explores the tensive side of celebration preaching through the lament of African American spirituals (Minneapolis: Fortress Press, 2012).

celebration, and in many contexts verbal and physical response. Though codified and mastered by African American preachers, revivalist traditions of many contexts will resonate with the form and respond well to it. More staid and reserved traditions will have to contextualize this form in ways fitting to the context and church culture.[14]

Cultural flip

This sermon form emphasizes a pattern in the teachings of Christ in the Gospels. The three primary central moves of the sermon are as follows: "You have heard it said...but I say to you...so blessed are they who..." The preacher begins with a culturally accepted, or common religious, teaching. The teaching at least initially is familiar and accepted. The tension is introduced, and the familiar and oft-heard concept is troubled, contradicted, or critiqued. The tension is felt more strongly if the listener is helped to accept what is good about the "you have heard it said" before rejecting it too glibly. As was the pattern for the Matthean Jesus's refutation of the Pharisaical teachings of the day, the "I say to you" is rooted in scripture's plain statements providing clear evidence to the contrary. "Blessed are those who..." gives space for the preacher to paint imagistic and narrative portraits of what life could look like lived according to the gospel.

The sermon began this way. "You have heard the phrase 'Blood is thicker than water' haven't you? That is what we often say: Blood is thicker than water. Those we relate to by blood are the ones who are there when we need them most. Our blood relatives will be there when coworkers leave, neighbors move, and friends leave us behind." This is the "you have heard it said" section. Upon development it becomes clear this teaching has been interwoven with the gospel, adding many moral requirements to it. Families should support each other in hard times. Children should choose family over friendships. Loyalty should be given first to the family. Family members should stay close to one another at all costs.

---

14. An important note for readers who do not emerge from African American contexts: above all else avoid any sense of characterization of another culture.

The preacher then shifts from one move to the next, saying, "But I say to you, water is thicker than blood. Have you noticed how Jesus responds to his family across the years of his life? It is disturbing really." Then after multiple troubling references to Jesus's immediate family the pastor asks, "In case we are tempted to believe Jesus was just unluckier than we in his family, have you noticed what he teaches regarding to family in general?" The sermon develops the difficulty many face in families. Without rejecting the value of loving families, it breaks open what it means to be family and validates friendship as "the family we choose."

The final move in the sermon begins with "Blessed are they who learn the art of spiritual friendship." The waters of baptism are elevated as a stronger bond than the blood of family. Good news is spoken to the abused, abandoned, neglected, or oppressed. The church is called to surrogate parenting, spiritual direction, relational discipleship, and simple friendship as a life of good news. Family is re-graced as a place where spiritual friendship, not obligation or shame, should be the central defining trait. The sermon ended this way, "You have heard it said, 'Blood is thicker than water.' But I give thanks today, that when we need it most, water can be thicker than blood, even among family. Go in peace, remembering Christ, who calls you friends."

One sermon form nearly defies any clear form. My students call it *the service is the sermon*. In this form the liturgical surroundings and the preaching moments become so intertwined as to be indivisible. The "message" is delivered by the entire service, not only in theory, but also in form. This sermon "form" seems to be a well-loved practice for worship leaders when a preacher decides to use it. Perhaps the reason is it forces earlier communication and greater cooperation with the rest of the service than many preachers are willing to give. The simple concept is to divide the sermon into discrete moves of a few minutes each. Then weave the sermon and other worship elements in and out of one another. The call to worship then may be the first sermonic move. A hymn, spiritual, or other song is carefully chosen for the thematic connection and two verses sung. Another sermonic move is shared, followed by two more verses and a responsive reading. A third sermonic move is given, followed perhaps by pastoral prayer or the confession of a creed. The service continues in this way until the final benediction, with each successive sermonic and liturgical move serving the greater message for the day. Testimonies, videos, the sacraments, and other creative interactive elements can all be included in service to the "message" for the day, presented by the entire service.

There are innumerable sermon forms possible for the creative mind. These are simply sermon forms tested by preachers, well received by listeners. They are listed here because they seem to emerge out of more than one text, more than one context or topic, and help the preacher rather than restrict the preacher. Though it is helpful to play with new sermon forms, practicing the same two or three forms multiple times until the preacher internalizes them accomplishes more. Then the sermon form will naturally emerge in sermonic work in the future. The sermon helps write itself as the fluid of exegesis and life experience pours into the vessel of the form. If it becomes a truly great sermon, it overflows the form defying a preacher's desire to give it a precise name.

These forms all serve to accomplish a greater end than a well-formed sermon. If preaching is what it can be, the church is sent as a worshipful community into the world with lives more in tune with the gospel of Jesus Christ. Instead of collective sighs of relief the sermon is over, there is expectation, inspiration, and hope for God's gracious rule in the world. The church is taught the life of faith, redeemed from damaging attachments, healed where it once was most wounded, and sent out as a liberating force for the least of these. The church shifts from bringing good news to being good news in the world. Instead of asking if it is time to search for another church, listeners wipe away tears of gladness saying, "Now that was church."

For Reflection

1. Take time to write down the sermon form of the last four sermons you have preached. If you do not know a sermon "form"
   they fit, make up a label of your own. Did the forms match

the message/passage in organic ways? Were they forced? Did the sermon seem to be released by the form or restricted?

2. Is there a form described in this chapter that seems to best fit a passage you are currently studying? Take the time to write out a first sketch of the sermon on that passage in that form. What is the current or logic of the message that presses it forward? Where is its tension, and where does that tension *lead* in the sermon?

3. One way of discerning the tension a listener will resonate with deeply is to consider common human needs and the emotions connected with them. Look up a human needs list such as the one kept by the Center for Nonviolent Communication. What human need does this passage seem to register, name, or diagnose?

4. Often a sermon form is discerned after the sermon is beginning to come to life. The sermon form has partial connection with the sermon as it stands. In these cases, the sermon form helps fill in the gaps to make the sermon feel complete. Is there a sermon partially built in your mind or files? Which sermon form does it most closely fit? What elements of the form are missing that are named in the sermon form? What components or insights from the passage might fill in the missing components of the sermon form?

APPENDIX A
Exercises for Practicing the Preaching Life

1. Copy or rewrite appendix B (assessing the preacher for contextual virtues) for your own purposes. Prayerfully consider ten to fifteen members of the worshipping community who might be able to provide accurate perspectives. Seek a diverse representation of your listening community: old and young, multiple ethnicities, balanced genders, multiple lifestyles, and include regular and less regular attenders. Have someone else anonymously compile the results. Talk over the results with a ministry mentor or trusted ministry peer.

2. After processing the survey of contextual virtues for a week or two, choose one area of apparent strength and one area of apparent weakness.

   - Which Christian practices seem most appropriate for deepening the more apparently strong virtues for you? Schedule time for engaging one of those practices intentionally in the coming weeks.

   - Which Christian practices seem most appropriate for strengthening the virtues in which you are weaker? Schedule time for engaging one of those practices intentionally in the coming weeks.

   - If you do not know how to engage Christian practices, to foster strengths or reshape weaknesses, search for a spiritual director or mentor with whom you can process a journey toward these qualities in spiritually vibrant ways.

3. Copy or rewrite appendix D (summary of historic Christian practices) for your own purposes. Your own tradition may adjust or add to this more general summary. Beside each practice give yourself a diagnostic number without allowing yourself to be deluded or shamed in the process. Score them according to your best perception of your last year's spiritual life. For each one, mark them in the following way:

1) no recollection of this practice in the last year,

2) rarely engaged this practice in substantive ways,

3) occasionally engaged this practice,

4) regularly engaged this practice (some practices can be more regular realistically than others),

5) regularly engage this practice with depth and joy.

Discuss the following questions with a mentor, spiritual director, or ministry peer:

- Do you notice any patterns in your engagement with Christian practices? Which patterns are encouraging and worthy of celebrating? Which patterns are revealing and worthy of prayerful consideration?

- After journaling on this topic, discuss what you think the reasons are for some practices being more regularly, deeply, or joyfully engaged than others. What insights might this give you into your own practice of the Christian life?

- Which practices do you *want* to engage in more regularly, deeply, or joyfully in the coming twelve months? Be wary of legalism or self-shaming. Focus on authentic desire.

- Who might be able to help you engage one of these practices more deeply and joyfully in coming months?

4. Using Excel or a similar software, design your own four-week chart of sermon preparation modifying the diagram in chapter 6, "Rhythms for Preaching Practice." Try to give yourself an at-a-glance breakdown enabling you to work on multiple sermons in advance, knowing what point in the sermon process you will be at each day of each week. If you attend a group of preachers for mutual support, share it with them to gain their insights and reflections. For the next few months work yourself closer and closer to this ideal pattern. Keep a sermon preparation journal in which you jot short

reflections on how the process is working or lacking for you and your ministry life. Rewrite the chart every year to reflect your growing comfort with your own way of practicing the preaching life.

5. Choose a passage for a sermon that is several weeks away. During the course of your regular life and ministry seek to read the passage together with persons representing as many of the following categories as you can:

   1) a young child

   2) a teenager

   3) a young adult

   4) a middle-aged adult

   5) a senior citizen

   6) a person with disabilities

   7) a person of differing ethnicity

   8) a person of very different lifestyle

   9) a person who does not profess faith.

   Ask them first for their help letting them know you want their insights, questions, and concerns with the passage. Listen without judging, debating, or questioning. Seek instead to understand and empathize.

6. Spend time in contemplative prayer, reflection, and journaling about the injustices your community needs to address. Injustice is varied and so ubiquitous it can be paralyzing. However, most injustices begin to overlap and intersect with others so that focusing on one or two engages a community in the whole over time. Choose one or two injustices you perceive to be most important for your community. What are you best positioned to address? What is most urgent in the culture?

   a. In the first month following this reflection, gather books, articles, and other resources helping to inform you on the complexity of the issue. Read scriptural passages addressing this form of injustice for personal enrichment and reflection.

b. In the second month, schedule intentional conversations with other ministers, community leaders, key staff, and lay-people surrounding the issue of injustice. Share your concerns and ask for their perspectives and insights. What is at the root of the injustice? What keeps efforts at addressing it from being effective? Who is most involved in your community and how could you partner with them? How might a worshipping community such as yours best aid in doing justice?

c. In the third month, begin to personally engage the injustice according to the lessons you have learned and the relationships you have built. Be sure to engage in personal relationships with those most affected by the injustice. Scheduling this into your month's schedule of activities is important.

d. In the fourth month gather scriptures, theological resources, and other sources to aid planning a sermon or sermon series addressing the injustice. Include conversations with partners and relationships you built in the second month to discern the best way to proclaim justice in the pulpit. Strategically plan the sermons to help your listeners move toward a desire for justice in this area over time. Remember you did not come to address this issue in a moment. Plan a journey for them over time through your preaching.

e. After a year of engaging the issue personally, prophetically, and pastorally, schedule a new set of conversations with the persons you have built relationships with over the year. Share your new concerns and ask for their perspectives and insights. How well have your efforts raised awareness? How well has your life, leadership, and preaching initiated others in doing justice? What hidden forces may be hindering justice still? How might a worshipping community like yours best aid in doing justice now?

7. Reflect on the summary of preaching's overlapping functions found in appendix C. Assess the ministry you are involved with for its balance of preaching's functions: teaching, saving, healing, and freeing. Taking stock of the last year of preaching, label each sermon with a primary and secondary function. The sermon may have touched other functions, but seek to discern the primary and secondary. Give primary functions a score of 2 for each sermon, secondary functions a score of 1. Do not worry if you have to force a choice, a pattern should eventually emerge. Add up the scores and reflect on the patterns. Which functions seem to be most often used, or least often used? Perfect symmetry is not the goal. Instead, reflect on the results and discern what needs to be done to address any undue imbalance. Does your own preaching practice need to change? Should others, especially those who might strengthen a particular function in ways you cannot, be given more space to speak?

8. For one particular preaching week seek to more intentionally engage the triple-step dance of preaching: prayerful contemplation, scriptural meditation, and experimental expression. Some find it helpful to set an alarm during the normal sermon preparation blocks. The alarm is a predetermined time to return to prayerful contemplation or to practice experimentental expression along the way. Instead of moving linearly from text to sermon like an unstoppable train, cycle through prayer, study, and expression over and over again. Afterward journal about what was most helpful or least helpful for your preaching process. Modify your practice to make it a better preaching life for you.

APPENDIX B
Assessing Contextual Virtues for the Preacher

1. Not Really True   2. Partially True   3. Mostly True   4. Very True

Centered Humility

_____ Actively seeks to learn from Scripture and others

_____ Uses others-focused speech much more than self-focused speech

_____ Uses a gracious tone (not shaming or condescending)

_____ Presents self as equal to listeners, confident but not arrogant

_____ Is approachable and welcoming to diverse others

_____ As a whole, our community seems to think the preacher is humble

_____ **Total**

Compassionate Empathy

_____ Accurately gives voice to the listener's emotions

_____ Speaks in caring ways demonstrating a desire to help

_____ Avoids pity or patronizing tones

_____ Avoids callous or indifferent tones

_____ Is aware and understanding of diverse others

_____ As a whole, our community seems to think the preacher is empathetic

_____ **Total**

Participatory Wisdom

_____ Engages the Scriptures and our faith tradition deeply

_____ Offers new and compelling insight into life with God

_____ Offers new and compelling insight into life with others

_____ Speaks from a place of deep involvement with the faith

_____ Is well informed and helpful for living a life of faith

_____ As a whole, our community seems to think the preacher is wise

_____ **Total**

Courageous Justice

_____ Regularly communicates value for diverse groups of people

_____ Speaks on behalf of oppressed groups of people

_____ Takes personal risks to address injustices in the world

_____ Denounces specific injustices in the world

_____ Guides the worshipping community in strategies for doing justice

_____ As a whole, our community seems to think the preacher is courageously just

_____ **Total**

APPENDIX C
One-Page Summary of the Preaching Life

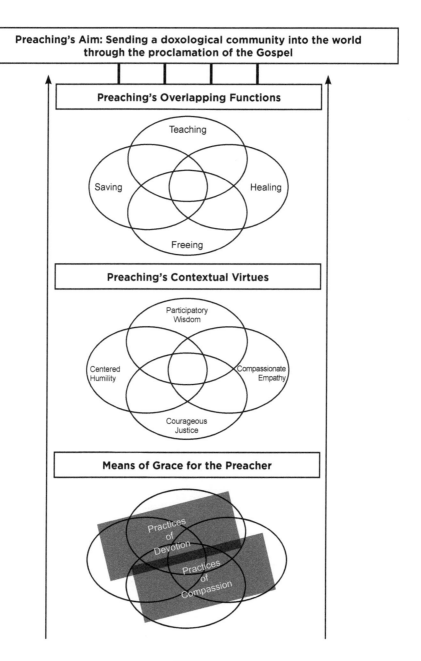

Preaching's Aim: Sending a doxological community into the world through the proclamation of the Gospel

Preaching's Overlapping Functions

Teaching

Saving

Healing

Freeing

Preaching's Contextual Virtues

Participatory Wisdom

Centered Humility

Compassionate Empathy

Courageous Justice

Means of Grace for the Preacher

Practices of Devotion

Practices of Compassion

APPENDIX D
Summary of Historic Christian Practices

Practices of Devotion

INDIVIDUAL

Prayer (contemplative and supplication)

Searching Scriptures

Fasting (food and other forms of self-denial)

Healthy living

Testifying/Sharing faith (offered or received)

Proclamation of the Gospel (offered or received)

COMMUNAL

Communion

Baptism

Family & church prayer

Christian conversation

Attending worship

Keeping Sabbath

Hearing the gospel

Practices of Compassion

TOWARD INDIVIDUALS

Visiting the sick

Visiting the imprisoned

Serving the poor

Generosity: Earn/Save/Give

Entertaining strangers

Caring for the forgotten (orphans, widows, immigrants/refugees)

TOWARD COMMUNITIES

Opposing injustice

Publicly naming injustices

Sacrificial acts for the sake of justice

Creating just systems

Civil disobedience

Identifying with the oppressed

Relinquishing unfair privilege

Reversing the effects of oppression

Abolishing oppressive social structures

Summary of a Four-Week Preaching Rhythm

A Fridays-Off Version

MONDAYS

Read in an unhurried pace the passage for three weeks away (sermon III). Prayerfully read the passage for two Sundays away and write down a few beginning questions (sermon II). Make 15 minutes of detailed observations on next week's passage. Then cycle through improvisational speaking, outlining, and writing this week's message (sermon I). Attempt to preach the sermon from A to Z even if stopping and starting throughout the day at different times.

TUESDAYS

Receive feedback during the staff meeting. Work toward a more final outline with key portions written for this week's sermon. Use improvisational speaking if necessary to gain confidence in the outline. Make at least 15 additional minutes of detailed observations regarding next week's passage (sermon II). Do some original language work with next week's passage.

WEDNESDAYS

Finalize and submit worship materials to the worship team (Keynote, Power-Point, etc.). Talk with your preaching group about next Sunday's sermon (sermon II), and do exegetical reading.

THURSDAYS

Attempt to preach this week's sermon from A to Z more smoothly. Begin improvisational expression, outlining, and writing of next week's sermon (sermon II).

FRIDAYS

Take the day off, mentally at peace with the sermon.

SATURDAYS

Preach from A to Z again in order to polish and/or shorten the sermon (timed). Prayerfully read the text for four Sundays out (sermon IV).

SUNDAYS

Preach from A to Z once more if you have time pre-service. If the sermon is already well polished, rehearse the introduction and conclusion alone.

A Mondays-Off Version

MONDAYS

Take the day off, mentally at peace your sermon is underway.

TUESDAYS

Receive feedback during your staff meeting. Cycle through improvisational speaking, outlining, and writing this week's sermon (sermon I). Attempt to make it from A to Z even if stopping and starting throughout the day at different times. Prayerfully read the passage for two Sundays away (sermon II) and write down a few beginning questions. Make at least 15 minutes of detailed observations on the passage (sermon II).

WEDNESDAYS

Outline and write the major portions of this week's sermon. Use improvisational speaking if necessary to gain confidence in the outline. Make at least 15 additional minutes of detailed observations for next week (sermon II) and do some original language work.

THURSDAYS

Finalize and submit worship materials to the worship team (keynote, etc.). Talk with preaching group about next Sunday's sermon (sermon II), and do exegetical reading.

FRIDAYS

Attempt to preach this week's sermon from A to Z more smoothly. Begin improvisational expression, outlining, and writing of next week's sermon (sermon II).

SATURDAYS

Preach from A to Z again in order to polish and/or shorten the sermon (timed). Prayerfully read the text for four Sundays out (sermon IV).

SUNDAYS

Preach from A to Z once more if you have time pre-service. If the sermon is already well polished, rehearse the introduction and conclusion alone. Prayerfully read the text for two Sundays out in the late afternoon or evening (sermon III).

CPSIA information can be obtained
at www.ICGtesting.com
Printed in the USA
LVHW050047290119
605569LV00005B/5